1989

Silk-Screen
as a
Fine Art

Silk-Screen as a Fine Art

A Handbook of Contemporary
Silk-Screen Printing

Clifford T. Chieffo

Reinhold Publishing Corporation
A subsidiary of Chapman-Reinhold, Inc.
New York   Amsterdam   London

© 1967 by Reinhold Publishing Corporation
All rights reserved
Printed in the United States of America
Library of Congress Catalog Card Number: 67-14153

Type set by Lettick Typographers
Printed by New York Lithographing Corporation
Bound by William Marley Company

Published by Reinhold Publishing Corporation
A subsidiary of Chapman-Reinhold, Inc.
430 Park Avenue, New York, N.Y.

All photographs by Clifford T. Chieffo, and diagrams
by Harwood Ritter II, unless credited otherwise.

To my wife Pat

without whom my life and work

would be meaningless,

and in fond memory of

my in-laws Bill and Lena Hurley.

Acknowledgements

I acknowledge a deep debt and extend my gratitude to the following people without whose help this book would not have been possible.

To Jean Koefoed and Sterling McIlhany, Director and Editor respectively of the Trade Book Department of Reinhold Publishing Company, for their suggestions, aid, and implicit faith in my work.

To Maryanne C. Colas, Manuscript and Art Editor of the Trade Book Department of Reinhold Publishing Company, for her generous assistance.

To Brian Sebastian and Ralph Logan, two talented young painters who devoted endless hours in my studio as my assistants.

To Alice Coote, my able typist who worked tirelessly with constant good humor and even went so far as to break her "never-work-on-Friday rule" that has stood unchallenged for 24 years.

To Neal Hall, a most talented photographer and technician who, working above and beyond the call of duty, produced the high-quality full page photographs.

To Harwood Ritter II, an extremely talented artist (who is also neat), for his exacting diagrams.

To Mel Feldman, my friend the lawyer, who led me through the labyrinthine intricacies of manuscript writing.

To Harold Rosenberg, critic, author, and scholar, for permission to quote from his Foreword to "Four on Plexiglas," and to Ursula Kalish, Associate Director of Multiples, Inc., New York, New York, for her guidance and information.

To Harry Baskerville, Assistant Manager, McGraw Colorgraph Company, Burbank, California, for his suggestions on the use of McGraw Colorgraph Photo Stencil.

To the Marlborough-Gerson Galleries, New York, New York, for permission to reproduce the works of Larry Rivers, Adolph Gottlieb, R. B. Kitaj. A special thanks to Brooke Alexander who considerately gave his time and effort.

To D. R. Swormstedt, President and Publisher of Signs of the Times, Cincinnati, Ohio, for his permission to reproduce the "pedal-lift" printing table from the H. L. Hiett book, *57 How-to-Do-It-Charts.*

To the Andrew Jeri Company, Inc., Caldwell Township, New Jersey, for their permission to use the data on their fine product Maskoid.

To Morris Scher, of the D.C. Silk-screen Process Supply Company, Washington, D.C., for his advice on materials.

To Leo Castelli of the Castelli Gallery, New York, New York, for permission to reproduce the works of Robert Rauschenberg and Andy Warhol.

To Ernest O. Gosbee of Washington Color Photo, Gaithersburg, Maryland, for the kind use of his equipment.

To my parents, friends, and especially Mike and Sunny Miller, who have had faith in my work since the beginning.

To Dawa Bosonow of Bosonow Printers for his time and technical information on the printing of the "Four on Plexiglas."

To Elliott Ephraim of Elliott's Books, New Haven, Connecticut, whose advice I always remembered to go to press "before the deadline."

and last but not least,

To my wife, my mentor, who erased, cooked, and loved — in that order.

Contents

C-1. DEMO II, 14¼ by 14¼ inches, by Clifford T. Chieffo, 1966. Medium: silk-screen. (Photograph by Neal Hall.)

C-2. DEMO I, 14¼ by 14¼ inches, by Clifford T. Chieffo, 1965. Medium: acrylic on canvas. (Photograph by Neal Hall.)

C-3. FRENCH MONEY, 30 by 32 inches, by Larry Rivers, 1965. Media: silk-screen and collage, eleven colors screened on 100 percent rag board, graphite gray screened on ⅛-inch Plexiglas with ten Plexiglas cutouts affixed to the surface. Collection of the author. (Photograph by Neal Hall.)

C-4. FRENCH MONEY I, 35¼ by 59 inches, by Larry Rivers, 1961. Medium: oil on canvas. Collection of Larry Rivers. Courtesy of the Marlborough-Gerson Gallery, New York.

Preface

This book, concerned essentially with the technique of silk-screen printing, is intended for painters and other artists who have already developed their own image and language of expression in another medium, as well as for printmakers, teachers, and students. My first ideas for a book of this nature came from my own experiences as a teacher and as a painter who makes prints. I felt so strongly about the silk-screen process being an intermediary between painting and graphics that I wanted to try to encourage my painter friends to explore this relatively little-used medium. Technically it belongs to the field of graphics because more than one finished product is created, but visually I believe it is closer to painting.

The reason that I feel so intense about the possibilities of the silk-screen process probably stems from my own predilection for painting. As a painter, I was in constant search for other image-making tools that would not burden me with their technical or mechanical necessities. Etching and lithography (with all due respect, some of my best friends are printmakers) with their chemicals, resins, expensive presses, and long delays in procedure, failed to satisfy my needs for producing a multi-copy art product. Techniques per se — the fetish of *some* printmakers — were never of interest to me. My orientation as a painter had taught me that the completed image that was created was the important issue in a work of art, not *how* it was created. I continued the search for a "rubber-faced" medium that would allow me to translate my ideas into visual terms without the medium imparting too much of its own look on the finished product. I found my answer many years ago in the stepchild of printmaking — the silk-screen process.

Silk-screen printing is a delight for the painter. There is no complicated equipment; the working image is not reversed in the finished product; a full range of colors is available for use including the artist's tube colors allowing for complete color accuracy in printing; the registration process is simple, making multicolor work possible; brush strokes and an impasto buildup of paint can also be duplicated; and last but not least, the silk screen can be used to print on any surface including canvas.

To demonstrate the potential of the silk-screen process, I purposely selected a painting of mine as a model for a print (see Colorplate 1). The painting, complicated in both image and color, provided a good test for the silk-screen process. The print was made without the use of photographic stencils which would have made an exact copy of the painting possible. Exact reproduction was not my aim. I merely wanted to exhibit the freedom possible in using the silk-screen process. Hard edges and flat color are no longer necessarily the norm for silk-screen work.

The Larry Rivers print and painting illustrated on the same page also emphasize the continuity between painting and the silk-screen. Here Rivers uses a variation on the theme of his well-known French bank note paintings and creates a print. In this silk-screen and collage print, eleven colors were screened on 100 percent rag board, and a photographic stencil made from a drawing and printed on $1/8$-inch Plexiglas with ten Plexiglas cutouts affixed to the surface.

Harold Rosenberg, in his foreword to "Using a New Medium," printed for Multiples, Inc., the gallery in New York that commissioned the Rivers, Guston, Newman, and Oldenburg prints, states:

> The bank-note motif, the deliberately messy surface, the fragmentary drawing, the use of space as if it were a wall or a blackboard, the bright oranges and yellow patches, the sulky green and pink make the "multiple" instantly recognizable as a Rivers . . . The medium [silk-screen and Plexiglas] has proved to be remarkably well suited to capture typical features of his [Rivers] paintings.

This work hopefully cuts through the profusion of technical jargon found in other publications and presents a clear, simple, straightforward approach to the silk-screen process. All aspects of the process are included; the building of equipment, translating an image into silk-screen terms, stencil-making techniques, papers, paints, and hints for the classroom teacher. From the techniques available, I have selected those that are most applicable to the fine arts. I believe I have taken the best of the old techniques and introduced some new, unique ideas, and looking toward the future, presented some little-used materials and forms that show promise for printmaking.

The book includes a gallery of silk-screen prints made by some of the foremost contemporary painters. My own prints round off the gallery selection and demonstrate the results of the exploration of various techniques.

It is my hope that this book will encourage other painters to explore silk-screening and will serve as well to introduce the medium to artists of all ages.

Silk-Screen as a Fine Art

Introduction

The silk-screen process is basically an extension of the simple stencil process. A stencil is any nonporous material, usually cardboard or metal, which, when placed over a surface to be printed, will block the passage of paint or marking material in some areas, and permit the paint to reach the surface in others. The benefit of using a stencil is its ability to reproduce the same design many times.

Printing with stencils was developed in ancient China and Japan where intricate stencil components were often held together and attached to the main stencil with silk threads or human hair. Now, many centuries later, the stencil is supported by silk fabric that is stretched taut over a wood or metal frame. The silk and the frame combined also provide a reservoir for the printing paint (ink). The paint is forced or pushed through the silk fabric with a brush or squeegee, and the stencil either "masks" (blocks) the passage of paint or permits its passage. This use of a stencil on a silk screen has developed into the silk-screen process. In the United States the process was refined primarily for use in the commercial sign and poster shops, and not until the late 1930's did its potential as a fine art medium begin to flourish. At this time the fine art result was dubbed a "serigraph (seri for silk) print" to distinguish it from commercially produced products.

I suppose that during the early years of silk-screening as a fine art a distinction between a commercial silk-screen product and a silk-screen print was necessary; but now, at a time when the silk-screen print is a recognized art form and graphic medium, the word serigraph is being used less and less. Artists and galleries are using the more descriptive term "silk-screen print" or simply "screen print." This book will refer to the product as a "silk-screen print" since the difference between an art product and commercial product is obvious. An original silk-screen print, I feel, is one in which the artist has designed an image specifically for the silk screen and has printed it or overseen its printing, and has verified his approval by signing each print in the edition.

Stencil making for use in the silk-screen process has almost become an art in itself. The prerequisites for a stencil are relatively uncomplicated: It should be easy to apply, easy to remove, and yet not be damaged or dissolved by the paint or its solvents. This last prerequisite pertaining to solvents is one of the most important. The artist should first determine what kind of a surface he intends to print on: glass, wood, paper, cardboard, metal, plastic, canvas, fabric, etc. Then he must decide what paint is most appropriate and finally, select a suitable stencil material. After the stencil material is selected, he may then choose any number of stencil-making techniques.

It is to stencil-making techniques that a large portion of this book is devoted. However, all of the salient features of the silk-screen process are covered, from screen construction to paint storage, so that the book will be a working tool for the artist.

1. Equipment

Having the proper printing equipment is a key factor in making satisfactory prints. Although all the equipment can be built with simple hand tools and a basic knowledge of carpentry, it should be noted that the major components of the equipment, or complete silk-screen kits, can be purchased at most art materials and silk-screen supply houses. Any painter who has stretched his own canvas and framed a painting will already have the necessary tools. They are: a screwdriver, a hammer, a staple gun, a square, a drill with drill bits and countersink bit, and a ruler. Canvas stretching pliers may be useful, but are not necessary. There are four basic components to the printing equipment: the baseboard, the hingebar, the screen, and the squeegee. Before you determine the size of the printing screen, you should take into consideration the size of suitable printing papers available in your area. You should also check the width of the screen fabric available. It varies from approximately 40, 50, 55, or 60 inches to as wide as 80 inches in some meshes.

THE SCREEN

Screen materials

Screen materials vary in cost and type, each having a particular purpose. The materials range from Swiss silk, American silk, Dacron, Mono Filament Nylon, cotton or silk organdy to wire cloth made of phosphor bronze, brass, and stainless steel.

The wire cloth is the most expensive, averaging approximately three to four times the price of the finest Swiss silk. Wire cloth is also the least practical for the artist because of its susceptibility to denting which may occur in normal handling. This problem does not exist in fabric materials because of their characteristic flexibility. I have, however, seen stainless steel screens used with great success in industries that need to produce thousands of printings of one image.

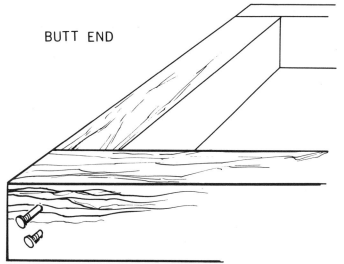

BUTT END

1-1

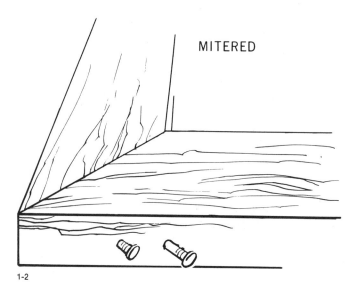

MITERED

1-2

1-3

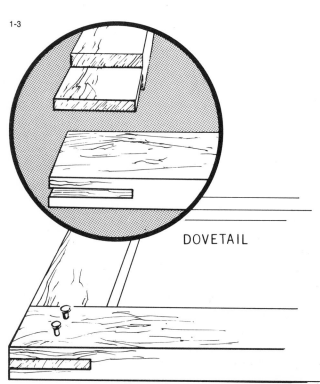

DOVETAIL

The least expensive of the screen materials are the cotton, Dacron, or silk organdy (suitable for use in schools. See "schools" page 112). By far the most adaptable and preferred material for the artist, however, is Swiss or American silk. The Swiss imported silk is slightly more expensive than the American, but both exhibit great strength and evenness of mesh count.

Silk and other fabric materials are graded in numbers ranging from approximately 2 to 20. The higher the number, the greater the mesh count or number of threads per square inch; therefore, the finer the silk, the lower the number, the coarser the silk, etc. Although the best size number is generally determined by experimentation and image requirements, number 12 silk is a good, versatile size for the artist. The more open mesh deposits more paint on the paint surface while the finer mesh is used for printing finer detail. Most fabrics are supplied in double weight, designated by a xx symbol after the number of the fabric. For example, number 12xx double weight fabric is generally preferred to single weight fabric. Even with the same number, the mesh count may vary slightly from material to material. The following table is an approximate list of silk sizes and their mesh counts that are generally available.

Number	Mesh count
6xx	74
8xx	86
10xx	108
12xx	124
14xx	139
16xx	157
18xx	170
20xx	183

Sizes 10xx through 16xx are used most commonly by artists.

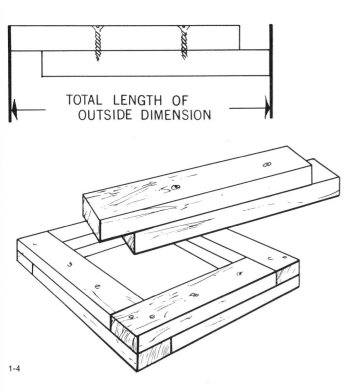

TOTAL LENGTH OF
OUTSIDE DIMENSION

1-4

Building the Complete Screen

Step 1 — Building the Screen Frame
Once the artist has decided on the screen material to use (hereafter I shall refer to all materials as "silk" for simplicity), he is ready to build the screen frame and the companion equipment. Since the smallest width of a bolt of silk is generally 40 or 50 inches, it might be more economical to build two screens at one time. For example, 1 yard of 50-inch wide silk will yield two 23 by 34-inch screens.

The best screen frames are made from kiln-dried finished pine, checked for straightness and freedom from knots. Pine measuring 1 by 2 inches or 1 by 3 inches will serve well. The artist can choose either a straight butt corner (Figure 1-1), a mitered corner (Figure 1-2), a dovetail corner (Figure 1-3), or, for extra strength, the laminated double cross and cross corner (Figure 1-4).

Whichever corner style is used, it should be checked against a square, joined, sanded, and further strengthened with angle irons attached to each corner of the screen on the top side (Figure 1-5). Screen door corner braces may be used instead of angle irons, but on a nonlaminated frame the overlapping metal sides of the brace have a tendency to catch paint and make cleaning difficult.

ALL TYPES WITH ANGLE IRON SUPPORT

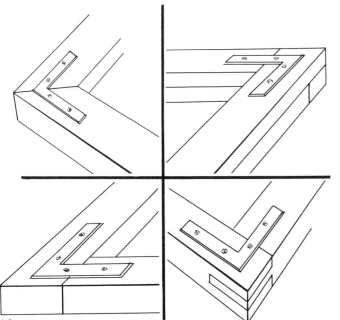

1-5

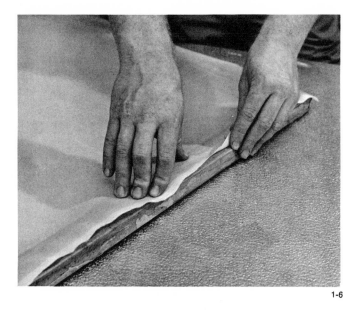

1-6

Step 2 — Stretching the Silk

The silk should be purchased to allow for a 1-inch overlap on all sides of the frame. The silk is tacked or stapled (stapling being faster and easier) to the bottom of the frame in essentially the same manner that canvas is affixed to stretcher bars. The following step-by-step procedure may be used:

A. Lay the silk on the frame with an equal overlap at the edges (Figure 1-6).

B. Begin stapling or tacking in a staggered pattern in the center of a long side (Figure 1-7).

C. After several staples or tacks are in place about $1/2$ an inch apart, pull the silk tightly to the center of the opposite side. Do not be afraid of tearing the silk as it can withstand great pressure (Figure 1-8).

D. Now start in the center of one of the short sides and repeat steps B and C.

1-7

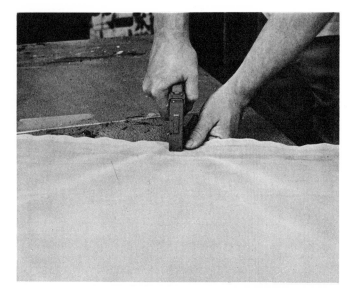

1-8

1-9

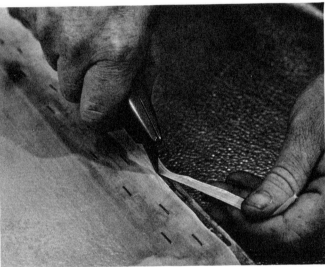

1-10

E. Continue stapling or tacking alternately from side to opposite side and work toward the corners. Be sure to keep pulling the silk even and taut (Figure 1-9).

F. Trim the excess silk ¼ inch from the wood edge (Figure 1-10). (For another stretching technique see "schools" page 113.)

Step 3 — Taping and Sealing

The silk screen is now ready to have the top inside and bottom (the silk side) sealed with 2-inch wide gummed paper tape to prevent the paint from seeping between the silk and the wood frame. If the paint were to accumulate and harden between the silk and wood, it could cause damage to the silk. To insure against this leakage of paint under the wood, the tape should extend 1 inch out from the wood onto the silk all the way around the frame. On the bottom side of the silk, the tape should also cover the staples or tacks. If you wish, you may provide additional space for the manipulation of the paint at the beginning and end of the squeegee stroke by having the tape extend $1\frac{1}{2}$ inch onto the silk on the short sides or ends of the frame.

Use the following procedure when taping:
A. Begin on the silk side or bottom side of the screen. The first piece of tape should establish the inside border of the silk, and overlap the wood $\frac{1}{2}$ inch on each end (Figure 1-11).
B. The second piece of tape should overlap the first piece and each end of the tape as well as overlap the side of the frame (Figure 1-12). Repeat for the remaining sides.

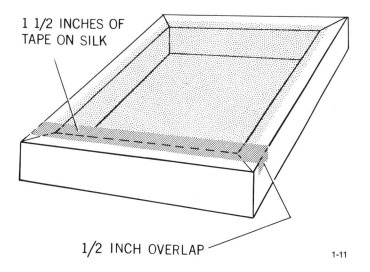

1 1/2 INCHES OF TAPE ON SILK

1/2 INCH OVERLAP

1-11

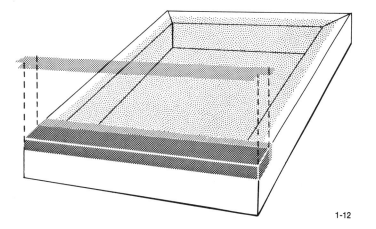

1-12

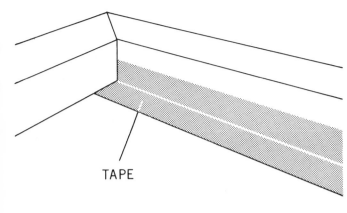

TAPE

1-13

C. Turn the screen over and cut a piece of tape to fit the inside edge of the wood frame. Fold the tape in half, lengthwise, gum side out, moisten and fit it snugly against the wood and the silk (Figure 1-13).

D. Repeat for the remaining sides (See Figure 1-14 for view of a finished taped frame.)

E. When the tape has dried, seal the tape, the wood, and the corner braces with two coats of shellac. This makes cleaning up easier and prevents the paint and solvents from acting on the tape. Shellac 1 inch of the silk beyond the tape to insure against paint leakage under the tape. (Note: I have tried sealing with acrylic-vinyl-copolymer [AVC] but the shellac still provides the best seal.)

Step 4 — Washing the Silk
Once the shellac has dried, the silk should be thoroughly washed with mild soap and water to remove the sizing and to tighten it further. After drying the excess water from the screen with a cloth or paper towels, place the screen silk side up on a flat surface until dry. If the screen is over 15 inches by 20 inches the corners should be weighted or clamped to prevent warping.

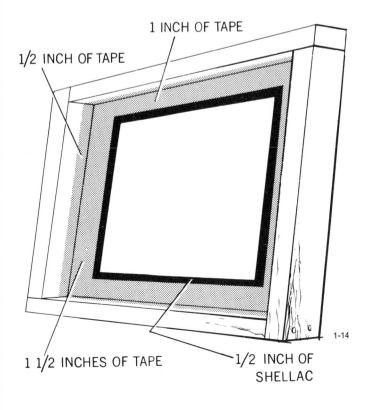

1 INCH OF TAPE

1/2 INCH OF TAPE

1 1/2 INCHES OF TAPE

1/2 INCH OF SHELLAC

1-14

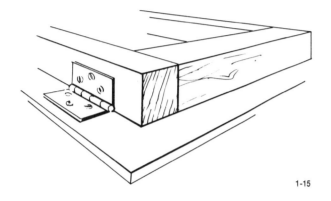

1-15

THE BASEBOARD AND HINGEBAR

Baseboard Requirements

The baseboard can be made from any smooth, unsplit surface of wood. Plywood not less than ½ inch thick is generally used. If the wood does not have a smooth surface, a surface of pressed board or Masonite can be glued and nailed to it. Occasionally for smaller screens, a scrap piece of plywood, laminated with Formica, can be found in a lumber yard at a reasonable cost and used for a baseboard. The baseboard should be cut from 2 to 5 inches larger than the frame on all sides. The surface, if raw wood, should be sanded and sealed with several coats of shellac.

Hinging and Hingebar Arrangements

To facilitate removal of the screen from the baseboard, "free-pin" or "slip-pin" hinges should be used. The hinges should be attached to a long side of the frame to prevent the paint from flowing onto the printing area after a squeegee stroke when the screen is lifted. The hinges may be attached directly to the baseboard (Figure 1-15), but this method places the hinge pin in a position that makes removal clumsy and difficult. Also, it does not allow for an easy height adjustment when printing heavy stock. A shim would have to be added between the hinge and the baseboard which would create undue stress on the hinge and possibly contribute to "registration" problems.

Rather than attach the hinges directly to the baseboard, I find that a better arrangement is to use a hingebar, which is connected to the baseboard by means of a flat head bolt and wing nut (Figure 1-16). Be sure to countersink the bolthead, so that the baseboard will lie flat. The hingebar should be made from the same stock as the screen frame and slightly longer than the hinged side. Check the placement of the bolts to be sure that they will not interfere with the hinge position or action.

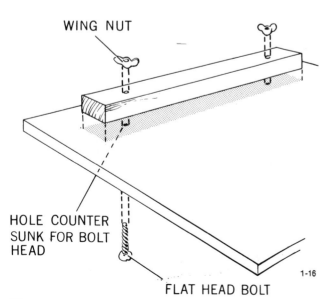

WING NUT

HOLE COUNTER
SUNK FOR BOLT
HEAD

FLAT HEAD BOLT

1-16

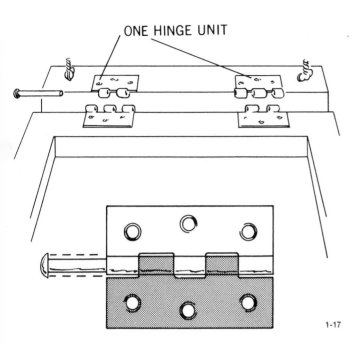

ONE HINGE UNIT

1-17

When the hingebar is in place, line the screen frame up against it and lay the hinges across the top of the screen frame and the hingebar. One hinge unit (i.e., two halves and the pin) should be taken apart and used for the frame and the other unit for the hingebar. In this way, both the frame and the hingebar will each have a two collar and three collar hinge half attached to it (Figure 1-17). Then, if another screen is to be used only one hinge unit will have to be purchased. The addition of two small holes drilled in one end of the hingebar provides a convenient place for the hingepins when they are not in use. When printing heavy stock you can adjust the hingebar to accommodate a shim made of the printing stock. Therefore the hinge level is raised so that the screen will make good contact with the stock during printing (Figure 1-18).

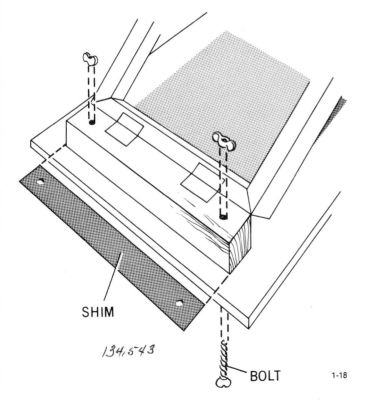

SHIM

BOLT   1-18

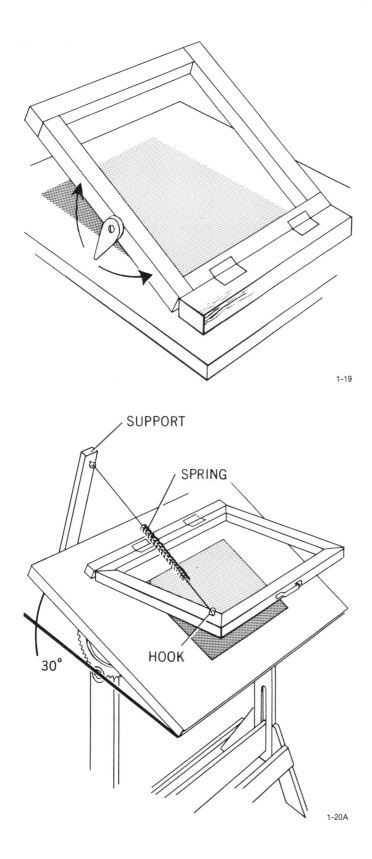

1-19

SUPPORT

SPRING

30°

HOOK

1-20A

SCREEN ATTACHMENTS

Props

Some method of supporting or "propping" the screen at a 40 to 45 degree angle from the baseboard is necessary to permit the removal of the printed sheet and the insertion and alignment of a fresh sheet. The "simpler the better" is the rule of thumb to follow for all prop attachments.

Two of the simplest methods in use are a wood or metal prop or a spring attachment. The prop type 4 to 7 inches long is attached along the side of the screen frame 6 to 9 inches from the hinged end. The prop should have a hole in it larger than the diameter of the screw that holds it to the screen to allow the prop to dangle free when the screen is lifted and to be dislodged easily by hand when lowered for printing (Figure 1-19).

The spring attachment type is comprised of a screen door spring and a vertical support. This type of attachment works particularly well when the table or baseboard is slanted during printing (Figure 1-20A, B). You can adjust the spring to hold the screen level during the changing of the paper, and thereby prevent the paint from running. If more than one screen is used, the spring can be engaged and disengaged by means of a small "cup hook" attached to the front of each screen.

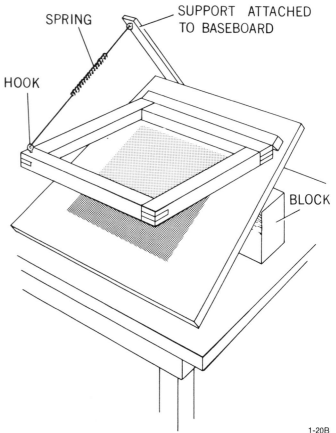

SPRING

SUPPORT ATTACHED TO BASEBOARD

HOOK

BLOCK

1-20B

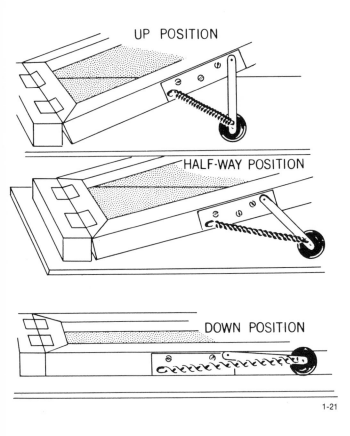

UP POSITION

HALF-WAY POSITION

DOWN POSITION

1-21

Many types of automatic "spring kick" legs or props can be purchased in silk-screen supply houses. They are attached by a clamping device or screws. The prop spring, stretched while the prop is flat during printing, contracts when the screen is released. The screen is therefore raised and held at the proper angle (Figure 1-21). A wheel is fitted to the end of the prop to facilitate this action.

Finally, to make the job of lifting the screen easier, a small handle may be placed on the front of the screen. In this way the screen can be lifted with one finger if necessary (Figure 1-22). In Figure 1-23 a special screen and table combination is shown that can be built if a great deal of printing is to be done.

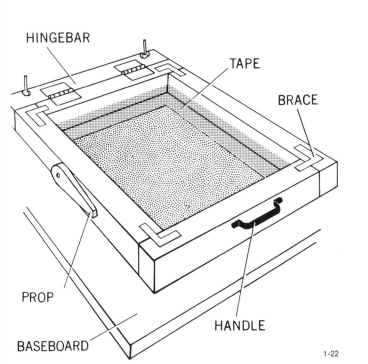

HINGEBAR

TAPE

BRACE

PROP

HANDLE

BASEBOARD

1-22

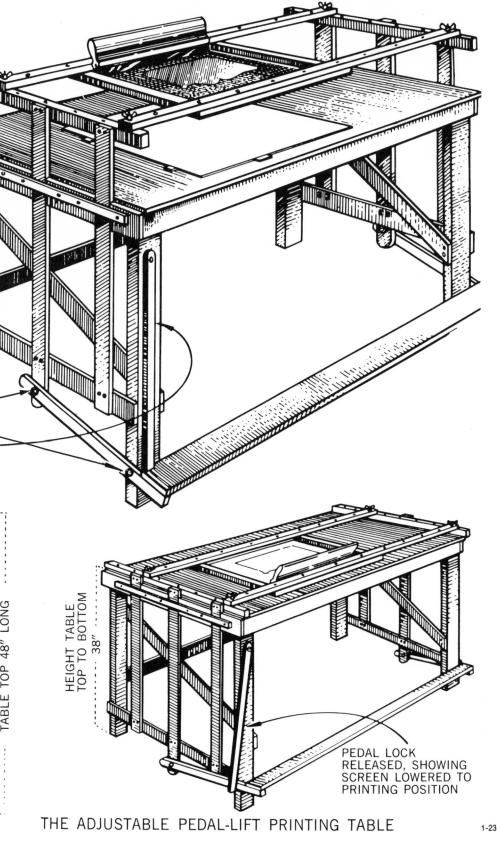

1/4" STOVE BOLTS
WITH WING NUTS

HOLES IN END SUPPORTS
FOR ADJUSTING
SCREEN FRAME
HOLDING BARS

SCREEN FRAME
HOLDING BARS, WITH
HOLES FOR PLACING
WOOD SCREWS FOR
ATTACHING DIFFERENT
SIZE PRINTING FRAMES

COMPLETE ENDS
SLIDE UP AND DOWN
WITH PEDAL ACTION

ALL PARTS UPON
WHICH ENDS SLIDE
CAN BE PARAFFINED
FOR EASY ACTION

CENTER UPRIGHT BAR,
TOP CROSS BARS
AND PEDAL ARMS
OF HARD WOOD

3/8" BOLTS WITH
WASHERS AND NUTS

HARD WOOD PEDAL LOCK
SWINGS OUTWARD TO
RELEASE PEDAL

PEDAL LOCK
RELEASED, SHOWING
SCREEN LOWERED TO
PRINTING POSITION

THE ADJUSTABLE PEDAL-LIFT PRINTING TABLE

1-23

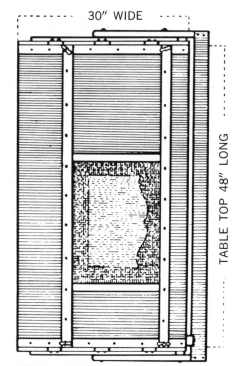

30" WIDE

TABLE TOP 48" LONG

HEIGHT TABLE
TOP TO BOTTOM
38"

TOP VIEW

1-23. Plans for the pedal-lift printing table, from H. L.
Hietts, 57 HOW-TO-DO-IT-CHARTS. Courtesy of Signs
of the Times Publishing Company, Cincinnati, Ohio.

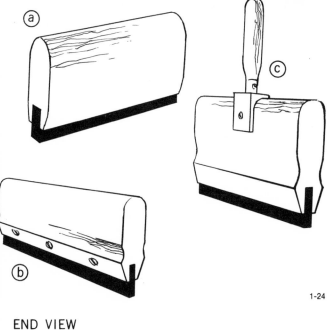

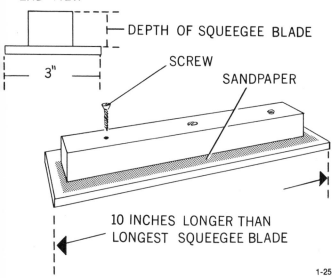

END VIEW

DEPTH OF SQUEEGEE BLADE

3"

SCREW

SANDPAPER

10 INCHES LONGER THAN
LONGEST SQUEEGEE BLADE

1-25

THE SQUEEGEE AND ITS USE

The Squeegee

The squeegee, the basic printing tool in the silk-screen process, is composed of a rubber or plastic blade $\frac{1}{4}$ to $\frac{3}{8}$ inches thick and $1\frac{1}{2}$ to 2 inches wide. This blade is set in a wooden handle and the length of both blade and handle is cut to measure. Figure 1-24 shows a few handle styles that are available.

The flexibility of the squeegee blade is measured in durometers. The range spans from approximately 40 durometers for a soft grade of rubber to 70 durometers for an extra hard grade. The blade that will give the best all-around use will be in the 50 to 60 durometer range; i.e., a medium grade to hard grade. Some companies also identify the grade of rubber by its color. Hard is gray, medium is black, soft is amber colored. Consult a dealer if there are any doubts as to the grade of the blade's flexibility. I have found that plastic squeegees, although about twice as expensive as rubber ones, are worth the extra money. They are easy to clean and rarely need sharpening. It is to be expected that all types of blades with use will eventually get a rounded edge. A rounded squeegee blade produces fuzzier prints and tends to deposit more paint through the screen. Sharpening the blade, however, is a simple matter. A squeegee sharpener can easily be made from a 3-inch flat board that is 10 inches longer than your longest squeegee. This board is fitted with a perpendicular strip of wood to guide the squeegee during sharpening. A piece of sandpaper or garnet cloth is attached to the surface of the 3-inch board and the squeegee is sharpened with a carpenter's plane-like motion (Figure 1-25).

1-26

Printing with the Squeegee

The printing technique used varies with the style of handle on the squeegee. For example, in Figure 1-24 models A and B are used with two hands, and model C with one hand. Before purchasing a two-handed squeegee, check the shape and depth of the handle for comfort when gripped. The basic printing technique used for the two-handed squeegee is to *draw* the squeegee across the screen from left to right (Figure 1-26), or from top to bottom (Figure 1-27). Model C, the single-handed squeegee, is *pushed* from left to right in one stroke and right to left in the next (Figure 1-28). Either style is a matter of preference, but in all cases the blade during printing should be kept at a slight angle (60 degrees) in the direction of the stroke. The stroke should be one smooth continuous movement; should it be hesitant or interrupted, a line will show on the finished print. The heavier the pressure on the squeegee, the thinner the deposit of paint. A few experimental runs will give you the "feel" of the squeegee.

1-27

Squeegee Blade Damage

Small nicks and cuts on the squeegee blade are easily removed by "sanding" the blade on the squeegee sharpener, but deep cuts on the blade will necessitate the cutting away of the damaged areas. The blade should be supported during the cutting operation with a thin piece of wood or cardboard and a metal strip or ruler used to guide the sharp blade of the knife or mat knife. Only cut as little of the blade as necessary to remove the damaged area. If the squeegee blade is damaged beyond repair, remove the nails or screws holding it in the handle and replace the entire blade.

Some final suggestions about squeegees are as follows:

A. You will probably find it easier to buy your first squeegee and then simply replace the blade when it is damaged beyond repair or can no longer be effectively sharpened.

B. Having a few small squeegees of assorted sizes will come in handy when it is necessary to print a small area or two colors at once.

C. The largest squeegee should be $1/2$ inch larger than the printable or open area of silk.

D. Squeegees should never be stored resting on the blade. A screw eye in the end of the handle provides a convenient way of hanging them when not in use.

1-28

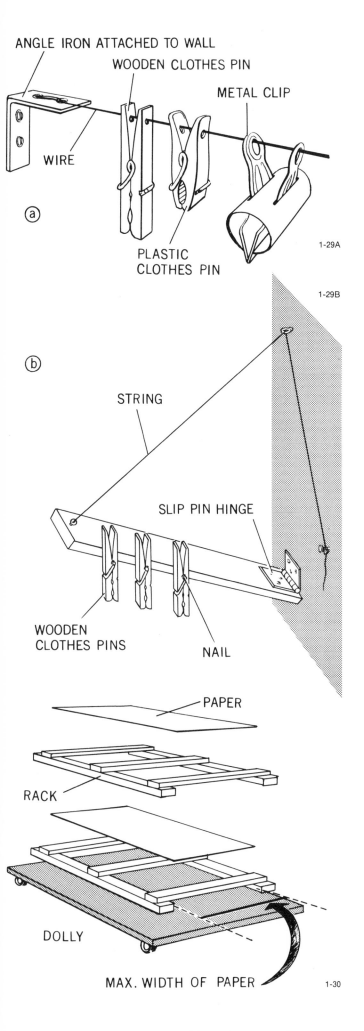

ANGLE IRON ATTACHED TO WALL

WOODEN CLOTHES PIN

METAL CLIP

WIRE

ⓐ

PLASTIC
CLOTHES PIN

1-29A

1-29B

ⓑ

STRING

SLIP PIN HINGE

WOODEN
CLOTHES PINS

NAIL

PAPER

RACK

DOLLY

MAX. WIDTH OF PAPER

1-30

METHODS OF DRYING

There are two simple prerequisites for the equipment used to store the prints while drying. The first is that the print, whether hung or stacked, should be kept wrinkle free. The second is that the printed surface should be free from contact with any object or another print.

The drying time of the prints may vary from minutes to an hour or more depending on the type paint, printed surface, and room atmospheric conditions. Since most of the inks or paints dry by evaporation, the addition of hot air will usually speed drying.

There are many styles of drying facilities, but only a few that are in common use will be described. The first and most elementary method is to use a smooth wire strung with metal clips or spring-type clothes. pins. The wire should be securely attached to a wall at either end with an angle iron. The wooden clothespins will need a small hole drilled through their handles (Figure 1-29A).

The second method is based on the same principle as the first except that the wire is replaced by a strip of lumber. The clothespins, secured to the lumber with nails (Figure 1-29B) that are not driven in all the way, are thus free to hang vertically no matter what the angle of the lumber.

If one-half of a slip-pin hinge is attached to one end of the lumber and the other half attached to the baseboard of a wall, the rack can be secured at any angle from the wall by a string from the top end of the lumber to the wall. Because of the hinged bottom, the rack can be folded flat against the wall when not in use, or it can be unhinged and used elsewhere by being supported horizontally across the backs of two chairs, counter tops, etc.

The third method is to employ loose racks of the same size that can be piled one on top of another. The rack is constructed of thin lumber in a manner that allows a space for the prints to be placed between the racks. The racks can be piled on a dolly and thereby made mobile (Figure 1-30).

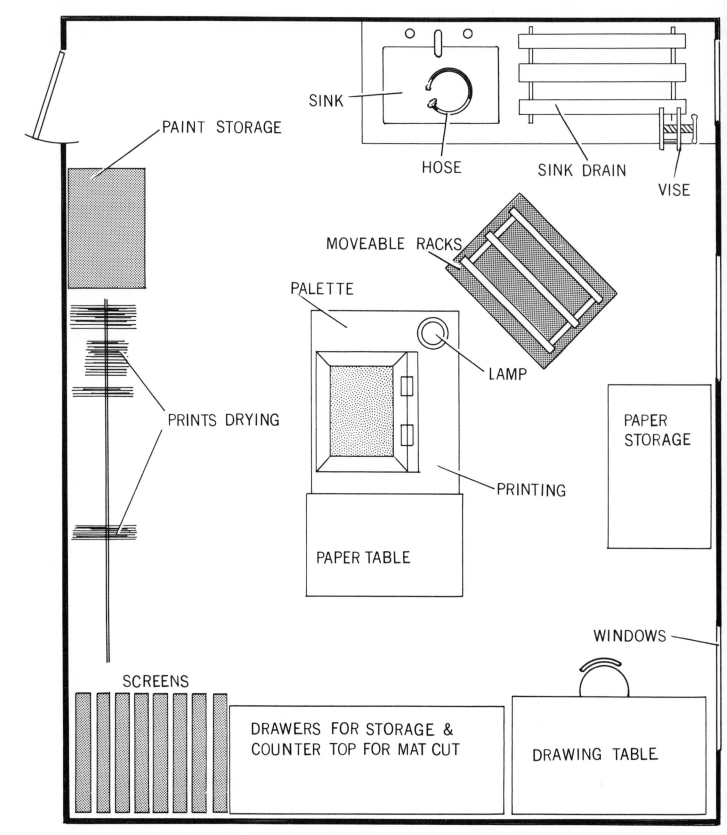

SINK

HOSE

SINK DRAIN

VISE

PAINT STORAGE

MOVEABLE RACKS

PALETTE

LAMP

PRINTS DRYING

PAPER STORAGE

PRINTING

PAPER TABLE

WINDOWS

SCREENS

DRAWERS FOR STORAGE & COUNTER TOP FOR MAT CUT

DRAWING TABLE

1-31. Suggested floor plan for a small printing studio.

2. Stencil-Making Techniques

As already stated in the Introduction, silk-screen printing depends on the paint passing through the silk onto the surface to be printed. When some of the printing area of the silk is "blocked out," i.e., the mesh filled in, the open areas left constitute what will be the printed image. The making of a stencil depends on using a material that will not be dissolved by the type of printing medium used. For example, if a glue stencil soluble in water is used as a stencil-filler, oil-based paint may be used as a printing medium. The action of the oil paint and solvents will not affect the glue stencil either during the printing or during the cleaning of the paint from the screen. Conversely, if a waterproof stencil-filler is used, a water-based medium may be used for printing.

Several types of blockout mediums are employed for general use: glue, shellac, lacquer, and special glue-like fillers manufactured by several companies. One such filler is called "Southwestern WaterSol Blockout," a product of Southwestern Process Supply Company, Tulsa, Oklahoma. WaterSol is resistant to all paints and thinners which are not waterbased, and is easily removed with *cool* tap water. I prefer it to ordinary glue because it is almost instant drying. When the term glue is spoken of, it must be a glue that remains soluble in water after drying. Le Page's Strength Glue is one of the better brands in wide use.

In the following sections I will discuss six major stencil-making processes and others, step by step: simple negative block-out, glue wash-out and lacquers, tusche wash-out, Maskoid and water-soluble fillers, paper and cut-film stencils, and photo stencils. Note: In all cases I shall presuppose the use of oil-based paints as the printing medium. Therefore all stencil types illustrated will be resistant to all paints and thinners which are not water-based.

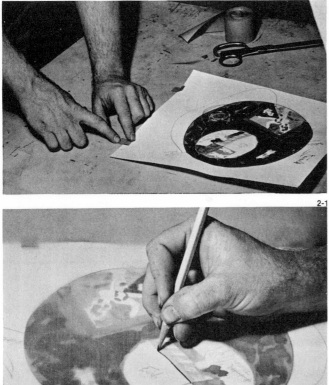

2-1

SIMPLE NEGATIVE BLOCKOUT STENCIL

In this method all the areas to be printed are left untouched and the remaining areas are filled in or blocked out with a filler medium. Lacquer or shellac may be thinned with the proper solvent (see Table, page 98) for brushing consistency. However, glue thinned with water, or a prepared blockout medium such as WaterSol (follow directions on the label for thinning) are preferred because of their easy removal with water.

Step 1 — Registering
Register master-sketch under the screen (Figure 2-1).

2-2

Step 2 — Outlining
Lower screen, and outline in pencil the areas to be printed (Figure 2-2).

2-3

Step 3 — Blocking out the Stencil
Disengage the screen from the hingebar, raise the frame above the baseboard, and brush in all the surrounding areas that will *not* print with blockout medium. Apply the blockout medium to the top side of the screen only. If any amount of glue should seep through the screen to the other side it should be brushed or scraped smooth with a piece of cardboard (Figure 2-3).

Step 4 — Checking the Coverage of the Blockout Medium
When the blockout medium is dry, check for pinholes. The screen is now ready for printing (Figure 2-4).

Step 5 — Cleaning up
Clean the blockout medium and the paint from the screen (described in Chapter 3, "Making a Print").

2-4

C-5. CIRCOLO GREELEY, 24 by 19 inches, by Clifford T. Chieffo, 1965. Medium: silk-screen. (Photograph by Neal Hall.)

2-5

Other Simple Glue Stencils

Simple glue stencils offer a variety of effects and can be made by applying the glue to a given area in any number of different ways. Textural effects, for example, can be created by using a variety of crumpled papers or a sponge to apply the glue to the screen. The glue can also be applied to waxed paper or other water-resistant materials causing it to creep and form unique shapes that can then be transferred to the screen by gently lowering the screen onto the waxed paper. Then remove the paper. Flat objects and surfaces such as wood boards and canvas can be coated with glue and then pressed onto the screen, but be careful that the object does not cause damage to the silk. Also, using various objects as stencils (Figures 2-5 and 2-6), you may spray glue onto the screen.

2-6. Detail of A HEAD IN THE HAND IS WORTH TWO, 26 by 20 inches, showing the results of spraying glue with an air brush using a doily as a stencil (Photograph by Neal Hall.)

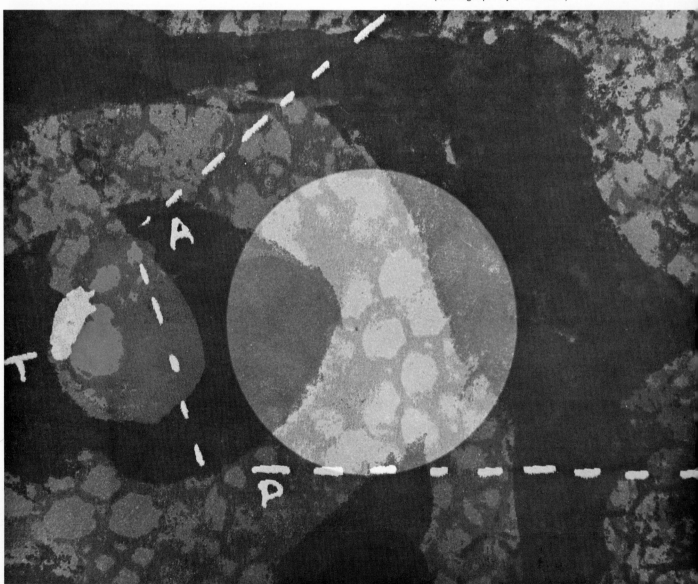

2-

C-6. THE BLOCK I, 26 by 20 inches, by Clifford T. Chieffo, 1966. Medium: silk-screen. (Photograph by Neal Hall.)

2-7

2-7. AUGUST 1965, 30 by 40 inches, by Philip Guston, 1965. Medium: graphite gray and buff, acrylic ink silk-screened on ⅛-inch Plexiglas, with brushed varnished coating. Collection of the author. (Photograph by Neal Hall.)

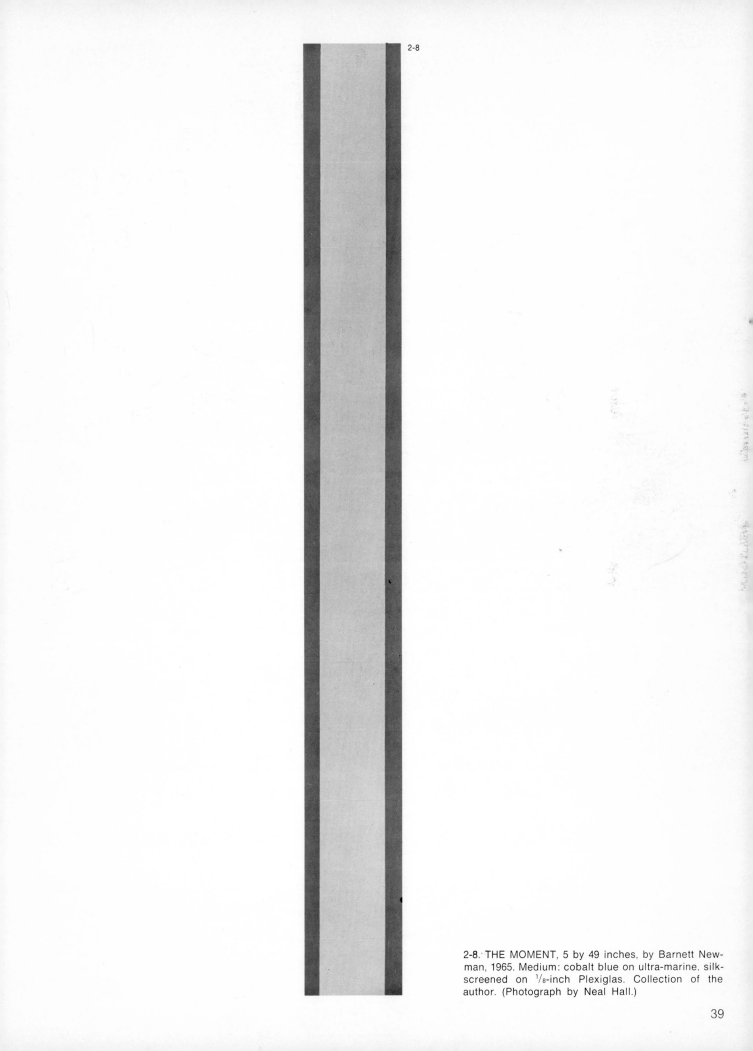

2-8

2-8. THE MOMENT, 5 by 49 inches, by Barnett New-man, 1965. Medium: cobalt blue on ultra-marine, silk-screened on $1/8$-inch Plexiglas. Collection of the author. (Photograph by Neal Hall.)

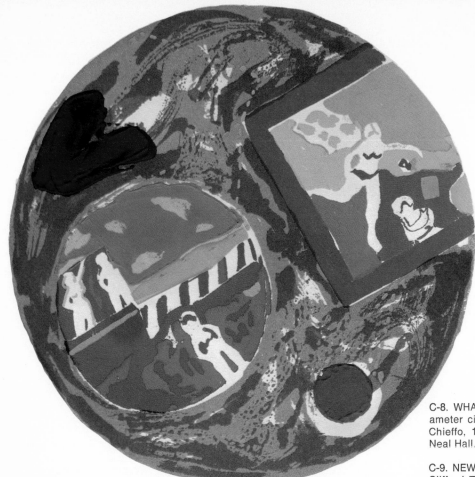

C-8. WHAT SHOULD WE CALL THIS?, 8¼-inch diameter circle on 15 by 11-inch paper, by Clifford T. Chieffo, 1966. Medium: silk-screen. (Photograph by Neal Hall.)

C-9. NEW ENGLAND SAMPLER, 20 by 15 inches, by Clifford T. Chieffo, 1966. Medium: silk-screen. (Photograph by Neal Hall.)

Tonal effects can be created by applying the glue to a damp screen. The dampness on the screen thins the glue. This creates tiny pinholes in the finished stencil that allow a limited amount of paint to pass through the screen. Because the paint area is broken up into tiny dots, the color appears to be graduated or shaded. The glue also can be used in a partial resist technique by applying a thin coating of light machine oil or mineral spirits to the screen. The coating causes the glue, when applied, to creep and crawl on the screen.

A variety of papers may also be used to remove some of the glue from the screen. Press the paper on the wet glue and then pull it off before the glue dries. Finally, the glue can be allowed to dry. Then, after being dampened in an area, some of the glue can be removed with a touch of your finger or a piece of paper.

Each of these techniques will yield unique effects and can be used freely in conjunction with other stencil techniques. Most of the effects are of a more random nature, but with a little experience, an amazing amount of control can be gained.

In review, it must be remembered that in the simple glue method, the glue itself forms the negative area or the area that will *not* print on the paper. The glue can be used as a positive image if the glue and lacquer technique is employed as described in the next section.

Two last suggestions are that, one, if a small amount of water accidentally gets on a water-soluble stencil, do not touch it. If allowed to dry, the stencil should return to its original state without any pinholes. Two, if the glue is difficult to see on the screen color it with watercolor paints to make it more visible.

GLUE WASH-OUT AND
LACQUER POSITIVE STENCIL

Glue can also be used as the *positive* area — i.e., the area that is printed on the paper — in a stencil by using the following method:

Step 1 — Brushing on the Glue
Raise the screen slightly off the master-sketch and brush the glue on the screen in the areas that you want to print.

Step 2 — Applying the Filler
When the glue has dried, coat the entire screen with an opaque lacquer filler. Use the instructions for "Applying the Filler" in Chapter 3.

Step 3 — Removing the Glue
When the lacquer has dried, remove the glue by applying water to the *under side* of the silk. As the glue softens, rub both sides of the screen briskly with wet cloths. The lacquer filler that is over the glue will break away and leave the former glue areas open for printing.

Step 4 — Drying the Screen
Dry the screen with clean cloths. The screen is now ready for printing.

TUSCHE WASH-OUT POSITIVE STENCIL

This method, more commonly known as the glue-tusche method, works on the principle of wax resisting water. A water-resistant (waxy) substance — i.e., lithographer's crayons, liquid tusche, liquid wax, or asphaltum varnish, is applied to the screen to fill in the mesh. A glue or a water-soluble blockout medium is then coated over the entire screen. When the blockout medium has dried, the waxy substance is washed out with turpentine, mineral spirits, or varsol leaving the water-soluble blockout medium intact. Thus, in effect, the paint will now print in the exact pattern created by the waxy substance.

The following is a step-by-step description of the tusche wash-out method using lithographic (liquid) tusche.

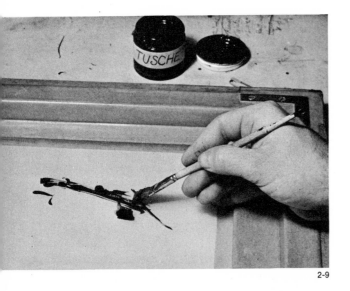

2-9

Step 1 — Applying the Tusche

Raise the screen slightly off the master copy. Stir the liquid tusche well. If the tusche is too thick, thin with either water or turpentine according to directions on the label. If the tusche is too thin, allow some of the liquid to evaporate by leaving the jar uncovered overnight; or pour some of the tusche on a blotter, and absorb some of the liquid by using the blotter as a palette.

Visual tonal or wash effects that appear on the screen by the application of tusche will not print on the paper unless the tusche has filled in the mesh of the screen. Apply the tusche liberally on the screen if it is to resist the glue. The tusche should be applied to the positive areas of the design (Figure 2-9). Check the effectiveness of the tusche frequently by holding the screen to the light. Two coats of tusche may be necessary in some areas.

2-10

Step 2 — Drying the Tusche

Allow the tusche to dry completely or at least until it is just slightly tacky to the touch.

Step 3 — Applying the Filler

Keep the screen raised above the master-copy. Apply an even coating of glue or water-soluble blockout medium by pouring a small amount on the taped area, never directly on the open silk (Figure 2-10). Then squeegee the blockout material across the screen with a piece of mat board (Figure 2-11). (Also see Chapter 3, page 92.)

The glue, if used, may be thinned by using one part glue and one part water. Prepared blockout mediums seldom need thinning, but if they do, follow the directions on the label. Two coats of the glue or water-soluble blockout medium may be necessary to insure a leak proof stencil. The entire screen should now be free from pinholes when checked against a light source.

2-11

Step 4 — Drying the Screen

Place the screen aside and allow the water-soluble blockout medium to dry.

C-10. EIGHT BALL, NINE BALL, ROTATION, 26 by 20 inches, by Clifford T. Chieffo, 1966. Medium: silkscreen on pewter-metallic paper. (Photograph by Neal Hall.)

2-12

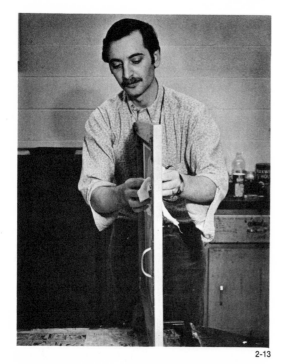

2-13

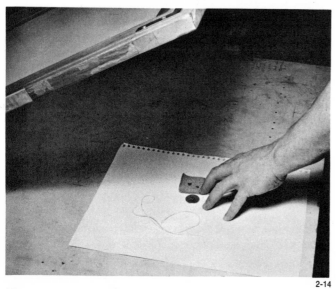

2-14

Step 5 — Removing the Tusche

The screen is now ready to have the printing area opened by removing the tusche. Place several sheets of newspaper under the screen and pour a liberal amount of mineral spirits, varsol, or turpentine on the screen (Figure 2-12). Using a cloth, rub the tusche until it begins to dissolve. Remove the top sheet of newspaper under the screen as it gets soaked with solvent and dissolved tusche. Continue rubbing the screen from both sides until all the tusche is removed.

If a few stubborn spots of tusche remain, they may be cautiously scrubbed with a small hand brush. This becomes necessary only if the glue coating was too thick and the turpentine was prevented from reaching the tusche, or if the tusche was applied too thinly and the glue allowed to adhere to the silk in the tusche areas. In cases where thick glue definitely covers the tusche, a small amount of water may be brushed over the tusche area and then quickly blotted with a cloth to remove the excess glue. Apply turpentine in the usual manner to remove the tusche.

Step 6 — Drying the Screen

Dry the screen with clean cloths by rubbing the screen from both sides (Figure 2-13). When dry, check to see that all the former tusche areas are open and the glue or block-out areas are free from pinholes.

Step 7 — Completed Stencil

The screen is now ready for printing.

Positive Textural Effects

Textural effects are made possible by using a lithographer's #2 crayon or stick tusche. Making a texture rubbing for silk-screen involves the same principle as making a rubbing of a relief object on paper. The screen is gently lowered onto the object; i.e., canvas, sandpaper, Ross boards, a wood plank or a wood or linoleum block that has a precut image, or any raised textured, embossed, or pebbled surface (Figure 2-14).

2-15

The lithographic crayon or the softer "stick" tusche is rubbed on the top surface of the silk filling in the mesh of the areas that *will* print (Figure 2-15). The screen is then coated with a water-soluble blockout medium in the manner described in the tusche-wash-out stencil method. The crayon is then "washed out" (see washout method of tusche, Chapter 2, page 45) opening the positive areas of the stencil. When dry, the screen is ready for printing.

2-16. Detail of A HEAD IN THE HAND IS WORTH TWO, 26 by 20 inches, showing the results of a lithographic crayon rubbing over a doily. (Photograph by Neal Hall.)

2-16

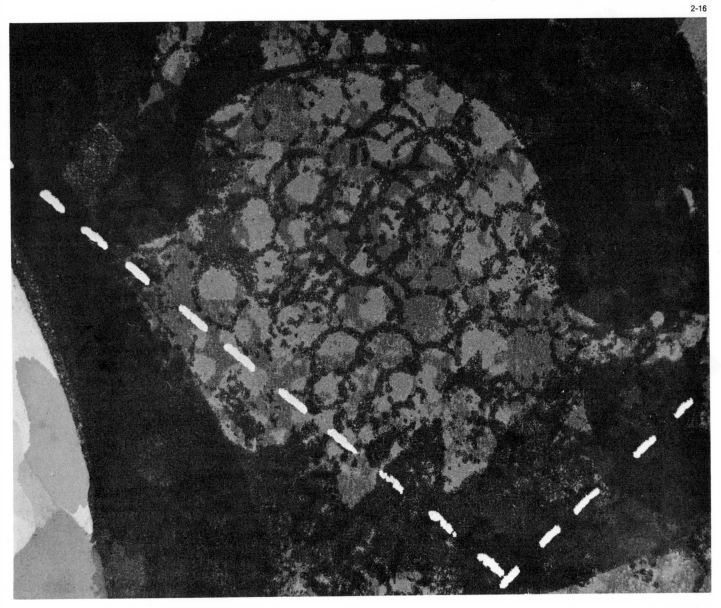

2-17. Detail of THE BLOCK I, 26 by 20 inches, showing the results of a lithographic crayon rubbing over
a textured table. (Photograph by Neal Hall.)

2-18. Detail of THE BLOCK I, 26 by 20 inches, showing a soft-edge made with lithographic crayon. (Photograph by Neal Hall.)

The lithographic crayon may, of course, be used to draw directly on the screen in place of, or in combination with, the liquid tusche. Follow the usual directions for the "tusche washout" method. The crayon used alone can produce a soft-edged stencil, yielding tonal effects in the printed color (Figure 2-18). Note: If you are working from the master-sketch on the baseboard, the screen must be raised while working with the crayon or protect the master-sketch with a piece of clear acetate. One important point to remember in using the lithographic crayon is that the crayon must *fill in* the mesh of the silk, not merely coat the top of the silk fibers. Always check your progress by holding the screen up to a light source to be sure the mesh is being clogged with the tusche.

2-19

Maskoid and Water-Soluble Filler, Positive Stencil Method

In this positive stencil method, the Art Maskoid (Andrew Jeri Company, Inc., Caldwell Township, New Jersey) or liquid frisket is used in place of tusche in the tusche-washout method. The Art Maskoid (different from Photo Maskoid) is a modified water-soluble synthetic latex. The dried film (insoluble in water and alcohol) is easily removed from the screen by rubbing with a piece of natural rubber resembling a crepe shoe sole or soft eraser. This easy removal of the Maskoid eliminates the necessity of using turpentine or mineral spirits to open the stencil for printing. The Andrew Jeri Company also produces a Silk Screen Maskoid which differs from Art Maskoid only by its viscosity. Silk Screen Maskoid is heavier in consistency and takes longer to dry. I use the Silk Screen Maskoid for covering large areas on the screen and the Art Maskoid for the more intricate areas. The following is a step-by-step description of the Art Maskoid or Silk-Screen Maskoid method.

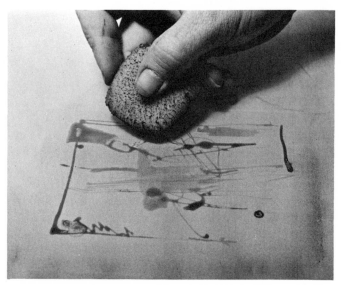

2-20

Step 1 — Applying the Maskoid
Raise the screen slightly above the master-sketch and apply the Maskoid to the *positive* areas (areas that *will* print) of the design (Figure 2-19).

Step 2 — Applying the Filler
When the Maskoid has dried, squeegee WaterSol, glue, or any water-soluble blockout medium across the entire screen with a piece of cardboard or mat board in the manner described in Chapter 3, "Applying Filler."

Step 3 — Removing the Maskoid
When the blockout medium has dried, lay the screen flat on a piece of clean paper and remove the Maskoid by rubbing at an *oblique* angle with a square of natural rubber (Figure 2-20). If the Maskoid is not easily removed due to an extra-heavy application of the blockout medium, brush a small amount of water on the Maskoid area and quickly blot it with a clean rag. Allow that spot to dry for a moment and then proceed with the removal.

Step 4 — Checking the Stencil for Printing
Check to see if all of the Maskoid areas are cleared for printing and that the blockout medium is free from pinholes by holding the screen before a light source (Figure 2-21).

Step 5 — Ready for Printing
Re-engaged on the baseboard, the screen is now ready for printing.

2-21

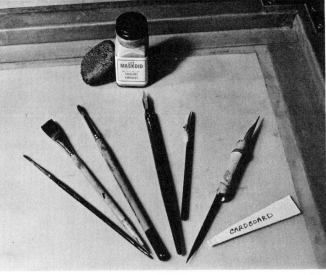

2-22

Tools for the Application of Maskoid

The Maskoid allows for a wide use of application tools (Figure 2-22). A bamboo pen, mechanical ruling pen, or a metal tipped pen may be utilized for direct drawing or line making on the silk. The tip of the mechanical ruling pen may need a slight sanding with emery paper to prevent its cutting the silk during the application of the Maskoid.

Brushes of all sorts may be used to apply the Maskoid to the screen. The following is an excerpt from the directions issued by the Andrew Jeri Company, Inc., Caldwell Township, New Jersey, on the label of Art Maskoid with regards to the care of the brush,

> "care must be taken to prevent the Art Maskoid from coagulating in it [the brush]. The following instructions will assist in maintaining a soft workable brush throughout the working procedure.
> 1. Wet the brush and rub it on a cake of soap in order to lather it (Ivory soap).
> 2. Dip the soaped brush in the Art Maskoid. Any soap mixing in with it will do no harm.
> 3. Add some soapy water to Art Maskoid if thinning is necessary."

I have found that a thorough cleaning with soap and water immediately after use will keep the brush free and clear of the Maskoid even if the manufacturer's directions are not scrupulously followed. If the Maskoid should accidentally harden in the brush, repeated washings with mineral spirits or benzine followed by a washing in soap and water should return it to normal.

Techniques with Maskoid

There are many techniques that allow Maskoid to produce a paint-like effect in prints. Some effects are suggested below, but the list is by no means complete, in order to encourage the artist toward further experimentation. Note: Substitute any of the techniques below for *step 1* of the Maskoid-Water-Soluble Filler, Positive Stencil method and continue steps 2 through 5.

Brush Technique. Maskoid applied with a brush is one of the best materials for producing a spontaneous, splashing stroke in the print (Figure 2-23). Although such a stroke is possible when thinned liquid tusche is used, the tusche will usually need a second coat and the original spontaneity will thus be lost. Art Maskoid has the perfect consistency for such free strokes, and seldom, if ever, needs retouching before the application of the blockout filler.

2-23. Detail of EIGHT BALL, NINE BALL, ROTATION, 26 by 20 inches, showing the spontaneous brush-strokes possible with Maskoid. (Photograph by Neal Hall.)

2-23

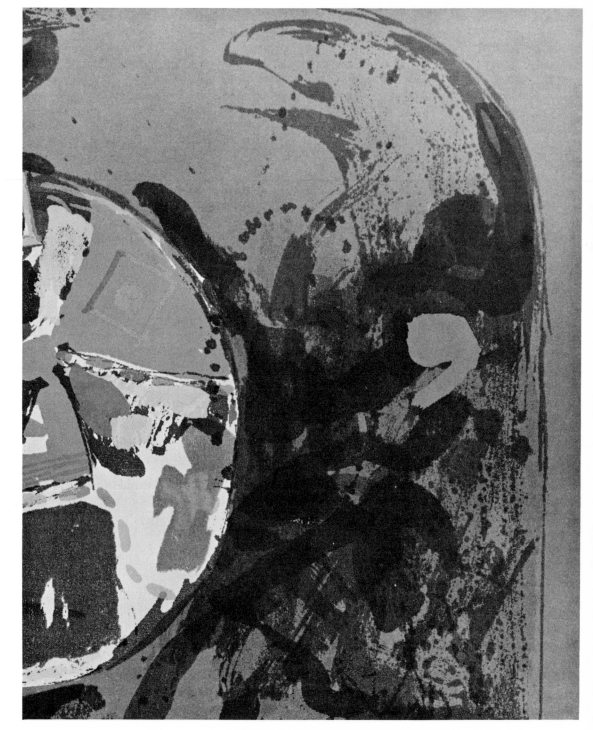

2-24

Cardboard Technique. In addition to a brush, a small strip of cardboard dipped in Maskoid makes a useful tool for emulating brush strokes (Figure 2-24).

Paper or Sponge Technique. Crumpled paper or a sponge dipped in Maskoid and printed on the screen will yield a rather unique *positive* stencil.

Partial Lift-off Technique. Apply the Maskoid to the screen with brush or pen. Before the Maskoid is dry, lift some off with a touch of the finger or a piece of paper. By using this method, you can achieve a tonal or soft edge effect similar to that obtained with lithographer's tusche crayon.

Partial Rub-off Technique. Apply the Maskoid to the desired area and allow to dry. Then before the block-out filler is applied, rub off part of the Maskoid to achieve a textured effect. Block out as usual, allow the screen to dry and then remove the remaining Maskoid to open the positive stencil.

Resist Technique. By far, Maskoid provides the best means for creating a *positive* resist stroke. Moisten the area where the resist effect is desired with mineral spirits. Apply the Maskoid to the same area while the screen is still moist. The slightly oily finish of the mineral spirits resists the Maskoid enough to cause it to creep and form a broken stroke (Figure 2-26). By the time the Maskoid has dried, the mineral spirits will have evaporated and the screen will be ready for the blockout filler.

At this point I would like to present a short case in favor of adding the Maskoid Method to the other major methods of stencil-making or at least opening the doors to further and more extensive experimentations on the subject.

2-25. Detail of NEW ENGLAND SAMPLER, 20 by 15 inches, showing the effects possible with Maskoid: upper left, line made with bamboo pen; upper right, resist; middle left, splatter with brush; middle right, crumpled paper application; lower left, partial lift off; lower right, partial rub off. (Photograph by Neal Hall.)

2-25

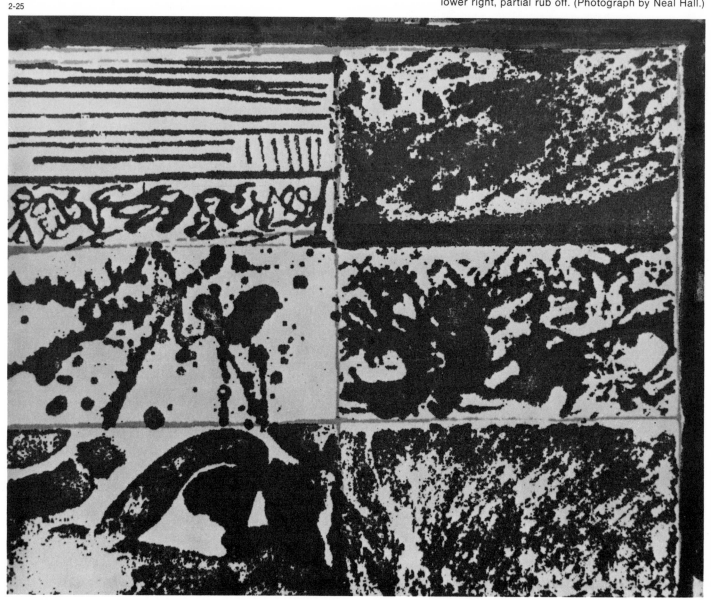

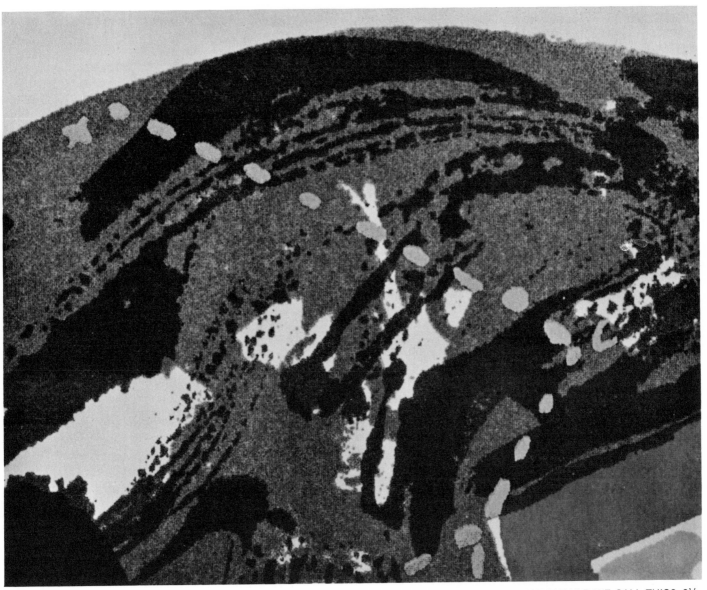

2-26

2-26. Detail of WHAT SHOULD WE CALL THIS?, 8¼-inch diameter circle on 15 by 11-inch paper, showing the results of Maskoid applied on a screen damp with mineral spirits. (Photograph by Neal Hall.)

First, Maskoid offers a greater freedom of application because it seldom needs two coats applied to the screen. Second, mistakes are easily erasable before the blockout filler is added. Eradicating an error with tusche means washing with turpentine (with little accuracy) and allowing additional drying time before work resumes. Third, the biggest advantage of using Maskoid is the total elimination of the "washout-of-the-tusche" step. Fourth, the Maskoid does not leave any stain on the silk after it is removed. The only time the Maskoid could not replace tusche is when the direct "rubbing" technique is employed with a tusche stick or lithographer's crayon.

One final word on the use of Maskoid: should there be any remains of the Maskoid in the screen after the removal of the blockout filler, they can be readily removed by erasing with a square of natural rubber.

PAPER STENCILS

Thus far we have concerned ourselves with stencil forms that are created directly on the screen. The major part of this half of the chapter will deal with stencil types that are precut, preformed, or prearranged before being affixed to the screen for printing. In all of the three types of stencils to be discussed, the principle is the same — the stencil is arranged and attached to the under side of the screen to block the passage of paint in the areas not to be printed. The paper stencil is the first of this type of stencil and, in some ways, the least complicated and the least expensive.

Many kinds of papers make excellent stencil materials. The paper should be nonabsorbent, thin, and transparent. It need be just transparent enough to see the master-sketch beneath it. Thin, white bond and tracing paper are frequently used. The thickness of the paper will determine the amount of paint deposited on the print. The thicker the stencil the heavier the layer of paint deposited. For further information on thick or "impasto" printing, see page 59.

Cutting the stencil can be accomplished with any number of knives made for this purpose. X-Acto, Naz-Dar, and Ulano knives and blades are in most common use. Silk-screen supply houses and art supply stores have many varieties of knives to accommodate any type of stencil cutting. A simple knife with a nonswivel handle will satisfy most needs. Unlike a mat-cutting knife, the stencil knife is handled like a pencil that is held slightly more upright. With a little practice you will find that the cutting action is simple and extremely accurate. When the blade becomes dull, sharpen it with a hard Arkansas stone. The following procedure may be used for cutting stencils.

Step 1 — Register the Master-sketch
Disengage the screen and register the master-sketch in the register tabs or guides.

Step 2 — Overlaying the Stencil Paper
Overlay the stencil paper on the sketch and tape it (masking tape preferred for easy removal) to the baseboard. The stencil paper should be large enough to reach the outside dimensions of the printing frame.

Step 3 — Cutting out the Design
Trace the outline in pencil of the areas to be cut and mark them for removal. You may, of course, freely cut the areas out with the knife without any tracing. Remember, the areas removed will be the areas printed. Proceed to cut and remove all the necessary areas. To hold a cut "island" or a detached piece of paper that is not part of the stencil proper (Figure 2-27) in place for printing, you will need to apply a touch of waterbase glue through the top of the screen

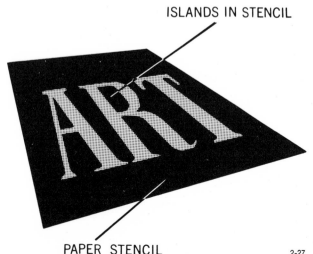

ISLANDS IN STENCIL

PAPER STENCIL   2-27

after the screen is lowered. During the printing of the first sheet, the paint will cause the entire stencil to adhere to the silk.

Step 4 — Reversing the Tape
While holding the stencil to the baseboard and without moving the stencil, carefully remove one piece of tape at a time. Lift up an edge of the stencil and affix a piece of tape with the sticky side up to the bottom surface of the stencil. Leave enough tape exposed to reach around the edge of the printing frame.

Step 5 — Taping the Stencil to the Frame
Engage and lower the printing frame. Bring up the ends of the tape and fix them to the sides of the printing frame. Before moving the frame, glue any "islands" in place with one or two drops of glue pressed through the mesh of the silk.

Step 6 — Preparing the Paint
Prepare the paint mixture, which should be thickened with transparent base, so that it will have sufficient body to make the stencil adhere to the silk.

Step 7 — Causing the Stencil to Adhere
Remove the master-sketch, insert the printing stock, and print the first sheet. Once the first sheet is printed, the stencil adheres and is ready for continued use. Naturally at the end of the printed edition, the stencil cannot be saved *on* the silk because the paint holding it will harden and clog the mesh. When the color run is complete for the edition, the stencil should be removed and the paint, and glue if used, should be respectively cleaned from the screen.

Three Further Comments
1. Water-based paints cannot be used with paper stencils very successfully because of the wrinkling that occurs when the stencil absorbs the water from the paint.

2. A second method by which the cut areas of the stencils are removed is preferred by some artists. This method is to mark the cut areas to be removed, but not actually to remove those areas until the paint is run through the screen. Since the entire printing area of the screen is blocked by the stencil, no paint will reach the master-sketch. When the screen is lifted, the stencil is firmly taped to it and the necessary marked portions of the stencil are removed.

3. "Islands" or detached pieces of stencil may also be held in place by cutting a hole or section from their center and then covering that opening with a piece of masking tape. The opening allows the adhesive of the tape to reach the underside of the silk and therefore the "island" to stick to the screen. The opening in the stencil "island" should be large enough so that the adhesive side of the tape will make adequate contact with the screen after it is lowered in place.

Special Effects with Paper Stencils

Torn and Absorbent Stencils. The artist will find a great variety of effects may be created with paper stencils. For example, if the paper is torn rather than cut, the resulting printed edge will be soft and vague rather than hard and crisp.

An absorbent paper such as model airplane or tissue paper may be used as a stencil paper with the intention of having the paint partially soak through the stencil and create a very subtle and modulated printed area. Using this method precludes a large edition, but once the stencil has reached a certain saturation level, it will print consistently for the remainder of the edition. With this process the first sheets are discarded until the stencil begins to achieve the desired effect. Naturally, there must be more than the usual amount of tolerance in allowing for differences between each print.

2-28. Detail of CIRCOLO GREELEY, 24 by 19 inches, showing lines made with a mimeograph stencil. (Photograph by Neal Hall.)

Mimeograph Stencil. A quick, convenient way of creating the appearance of a line drawing, typed words, or letters in the print can be achieved by using a mimeograph stencil as a paper stencil for your silk screen. The stencil should be prepared according to the prescribed method as if it were to be used in a mimeograph machine. This means that the stencil may be typed or drawn on directly with special tools that create a variety of lines when used in combination with an embossed or textured plate placed beneath the stencil. When the stencil is in satisfactory form the stencil sheet or vellum sheet should be torn from the support sheets and placed aside until the screen is prepared to receive the stencil.

The screen is prepared by blocking out a border around the area that will be covered by the mimeograph stencil with glue, lacquer or blockout filler. When this border is dry, the stencil is placed on the baseboard, the screen lowered, and during the first squeegee printing, it adheres to the silk. Any space left between the stencil and the border can be covered with tape. The screen is now ready for continued printing. Since the stencil material will eventually begin to absorb the paint solvents, large editions are not possible unless new stencils periodically replace the old.

Impasto Effect. Thick or impasto layers of paint are also possible with silk-screen. Although impasto effects in silk-screened prints were formerly frowned upon by printmakers claiming that the effect was not following the "honesty to materials" approach, in contemporary painting, printmaking, and sculpture many of those former values have been reversed. Prints may vary from low relief to actual three-dimensional shapes, paintings are employing real objects and are created on shaped canvases, wood sculpture is made to look like plastic, and fiber glass sculpture made to look like wood. Thus through creative use, materials are being stretched to their maximum potential.

Although impasto techniques are usually considered under a separate classification, I will discuss them here because paper or mat board stencils are used in some of the methods. Since impasto depends upon depositing a heavy layer of paint, using a more open or coarser mesh screen is desirable. A 10xx to 12xx mesh screen will allow more paint to be deposited on the printed surface. In addition, some minor variations can be created by squeegee pressure; that is, less pressure deposits more paint, more pressure less paint. For building heavier layers and more pronounced textural effects, however, other methods are needed.

Some paints, especially enamels, naturally deposit a heavy layer of pigment. By using these paints, combined with *many* overprintings of the same stencil,

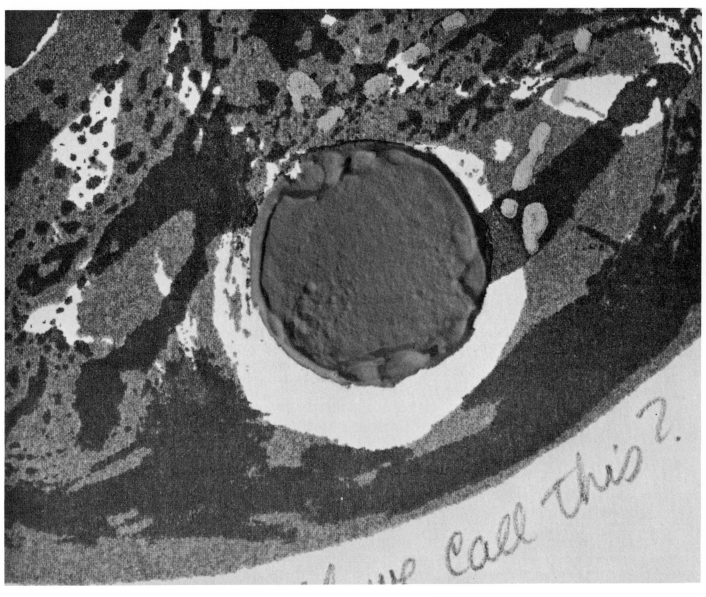

2-29. Detail of WHAT SHOULD WE CALL THIS?, 8¹/₄-inch diameter circle on 15 by 11-inch paper, showing a detail of an impasto area. (Photograph by Neal Hall.)

quite a noticeable build-up can be achieved. This method works well with any stencil type, including those with a relatively intricate image. For more simple, larger areas, the following technique works well, especially if you do not ordinarily have enamel paints on hand.

A paper stencil is used, but heavy paper or cardboard is substituted for the usual thin stencil paper. The regular screen paint is thickened with household corn starch until it does not run on the palette and has the general consistency of sour cream. The paint is then slowly and evenly squeegeed across the screen. This action should deposit a layer of paint the approximate thickness of the stencil material. A thick stencil material will cause the paint layer to

2-30. PALATIAL, 17 by 17 inches, by Josef Albers. Medium: silk-screen. A three color print using hand-cut stencils. Collection of the author. (Photograph by Neal Hall.)

have a considerably textured surface. This surface texture will vary slightly in each print, but the shape should remain constant.

The stencil should be checked frequently to see that the heavy deposit of paint is not beginning to harden and to clog the mesh or spread beyond the prescribed printing area. If any of the above conditions exist, the paint should be carefully cleaned from the trouble spots with the proper solvent.

The last method does not utilize a thick stencil on the screen and/or thickened or enamel paint. Cardboard, cloth, or thin textured objects such as screening, burlap, string, and sandpaper may be glued with rubber cement to the baseboard to create an uneven surface beneath the printing paper. The printing paper, a lightweight stock, is then registered in the usual manner. This time the creation of the textured effect will necessitate the use of transparent colors. The paint should be mixed with transparent base or extender so that even opaque colors will become more transparent. When the paint is squeegeed across the screen, a heavier layer of color will be deposited in the valleys between the raised objects on the baseboard, and a thinner layer deposited as the squeegee crosses their surfaces. The printed result will create a *visual* texture much like that of a "rubbing" rather than an actual physical, thick layer of texture.

The characteristic of transparent colors to darken when they fill in the valleys created by the object or collage surface on the baseboard can be utilized by printing on a "rough" or textured surface paper. Here again the color would be darker in the valleys of the paper's texture, only in this case the light and dark effect would be more consistent. In either case, consistent squeegee pressure during printing is the key to having only minor variations among prints.

All of the above techniques require a little more effort and preparation, but the results can be very rewarding especially when these techniques are used in combination with other stencil types. With a growing interest in contemporary art for the "unflat" print, I am sure that artists will give more attention to the impasto techniques of silk-screen printing.

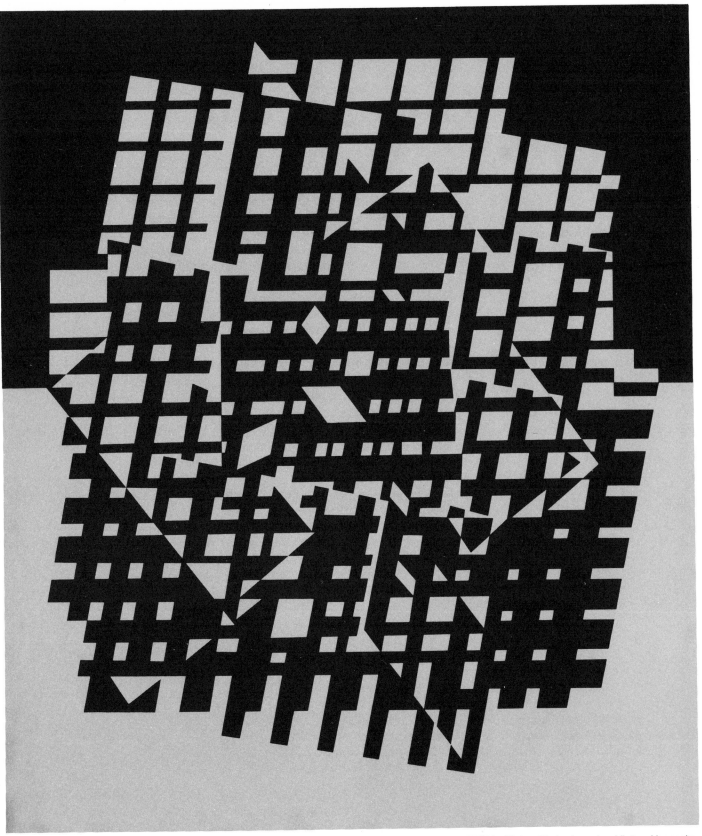

2-31. IXION, 26 by 20 inches, by Victor Vasarely. Collection of the author. (Photograph by Neal Hall.)

FILM STENCILS

Film stencils are composed of a very thin sheet of lacquer laminated to, and supported by, a backing of paper or plastic. The design is cut from the lacquer layer, the film is then adhered to the underside of the silk and the paper or plastic backing removed. Where the parts of the lacquer film have been cut and removed, the mesh remains open and the remaining portions of the lacquer film block the passage of paint through the mesh and constitute the stencil. The principle involved is the same as in paper stencils — the difference is in the materials, preparation, and adhering process.

The lacquer films made are designed to be used with all oil-based and water-based paints. Special water-soluble films are designed for use with lacquer or vinyl-based paints. These films are used in the same manner as the lacquer-soluble films, except water is used as an adhering fluid rather than a lacquer solvent. The various types of film are sold under different trade names. Nu-Film, Profilm, Craftint, and Ulano products each offer film for a wide variety of uses. The adhering fluid and film-removal solvent in each case should correspond to the film manufacturer's recommendations. The supplier of the film will generally supply the adhering fluid and solvent as well.

The following step-by-step procedure is generalized to include most films, but here again specific manufacturer's instructions, if any, should be consulted. Film stencils are used for the most part when fine detail and crisp, sharp edges are desired in the print (Figure 2-31). They are also extremely durable and capable of printing details sharply for very large editions. The possibilities of the film stencil is limited only by the dexterity of the person cutting the stencil.

Step 1 — Registering the Master-Sketch
Position the master-sketch under the screen and attach the register tabs or guides in the usual manner.

Step 2 — Taping the Film to the Master-Sketch
Cut a piece of film several inches larger than the design on the master-sketch and tape it securely, lacquer side or shiny side up, to the master-sketch (Figure 2-32). The master-sketch with film attached can now be moved to a cutting table or the screen can be disengaged and the baseboard used as the cutting table.

Step 3 — Cutting out the Design
To cut out the areas to be printed, use a X-acto or similar type blade held in the "pencil" manner as described in the cutting process for paper stencils. The object in this case is to cut *only* the lacquer film and *not* the paper or plastic backing. At every intersection of two lines, the lines should "cross-cut" or "over-cut" each other so that the resulting areas will

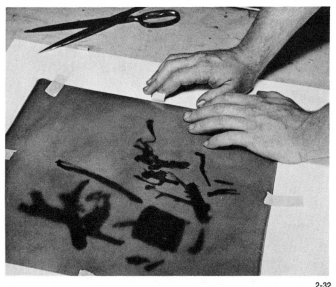

2-32

2-33

2-34

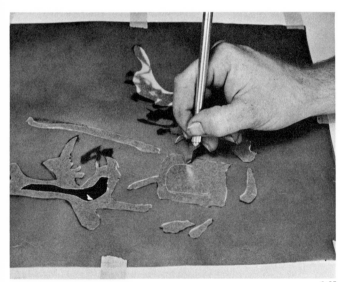

2-35

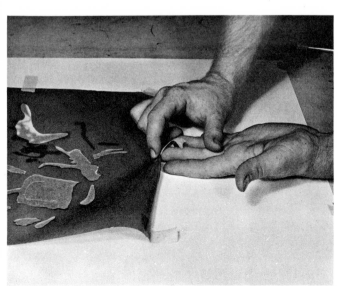

2-36

be easily removed. This is important even for the smallest area or the thinnest line (Figure 2-33). The small "over-cut" lines will be automatically sealed together during the adhering process. There are several cutting tools on the market designed for specific uses such as an adjustable circle cutter for cutting circles, a swivel blade cutter for cutting curves and a double blade cutter for cutting two lines simultaneously, which can be bought when the need arises.

Step 4 — Removing the Cut Pieces

Once all the designated areas are cut, they can be removed by carefully lifting a corner of the film with the knife blade and while holding the film against the blade with the left forefinger, peeling it off the backing (Figure 2-34). After all the lacquer film areas have been removed, any large areas of the paper backing left without the lacquer film should have some openings cut into them. These openings provide for the circulation of air during the adhering process (Figure 2-35).

Step 5 — Checking the Open Areas

Check the areas to be printed to see that they are clear of any unwanted scraps or particles of lacquer film.

Step 6 — Reversing the Tape

Re-register the master-sketch and the stencil on the baseboard. Carefully, *and without moving the stencil film*, remove the tape from the top of the film, one piece at a time, and slip it between the master-sketch and the bottom of the film. Then attach the tape to the paper or plastic backing with the sticky side facing up (Figure 2-36). When all the tape is reversed in this manner, carefully lower the clean screen onto the film. Make sure that the tape has made good contact with the underside of the silk.

Step 7 — Padding the Baseboard

Lift the screen with the film attached and remove the master-sketch. Place a sheet of newspaper or a piece of thick cardboard on the baseboard directly below the film area. The newspaper or cardboard is used to insure proper and thorough contact between the film and the silk. The newspaper or cardboard should not extend under the wood frame as it would prevent the screen from lying flat on the baseboard.

Step 8 — Causing the Film to Adhere

For the adhering process two lint-free cloths should be balled up; one will be used to apply the adhering liquid, the other to dry the stencil. Properly applied, the adhering fluid should dissolve the lacquer film just enough for it to adhere to the silk. Too much fluid will dissolve it completely or cause the cut edge to be blurry.

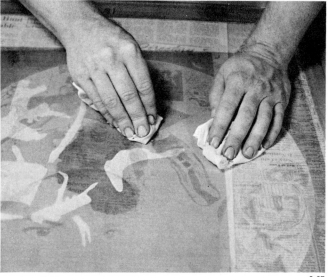

2-37

There are two places on the stencil where the artist can begin the adhering process to prevent the film from wrinkling — one place to start is in the center, from which you work out toward the corners; the other place to start is in one corner, from which you work across the film. Either way is a matter of personal preference.

Begin the adhering process by soaking and wringing out one cloth with adhering fluid. Apply the moist cloth to the top side of the screen and dampen a small area of film. Immediately rub this area briskly with the dry cloth to remove the excess fluid; continue rubbing until all the fluid has evaporated. The amount of the film that has adhered will appear a darker color on the silk. Repeat this process on adjacent areas until the entire film has adhered. Allow to dry (Figure 2-37).

Step 9 — Removing the Backing
When the silk is completely dry, raise the screen and remove the tape. Next, carefully lift one corner of the backing and begin to peel it away from the film. The backing should remove easily and completely (Figure 2-38). If you notice an area of film coming off with the backing, carefully return the backing into place, then lower the screen. Check to see that good contact is being made between the film and silk, and adhere that area again by repeating step 8.

Step 10 — Blocking out the Border
If the film does not cover the entire open mesh of the screen, block out the remaining border with glue, prepared filler, lacquer, or paper attached to the underside of the screen (Figure 2-39). The screen is now ready for printing.

2-38

2-39

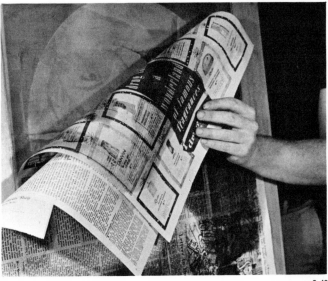

2-40

Step 11 — Removing the Film after Printing

When the printing of the stencil is completed for the edition and the paint has been cleaned from the screen, the film can be removed in the following manner. Place several sheets of newspaper underneath the screen. The cleaning may be done on the baseboard with the screen disengaged from the hinges or it may be moved to a separate area. Pour a liberal amount of film solvent (remover) on the top side of the screen and let it soak there for a few minutes and then begin rubbing with a clean cloth. After the solvent has been spread over the entire film area and rubbed, lift the screen and remove the top layers of newspaper. Most of the film should come off with the newspaper (Figure 2-40). This process can be repeated until only a few spots are left. The remaining portions of the film can be removed by propping the screen up in a wood vise and rubbing it simultaneously on both sides with cloths saturated with solvent. Set the screen aside and let it dry.

Some final notes on the use of cut-film stencils are included here for your edification.

I find it very handy to save all the film scraps in a jar, and when I have collected a fair amount, I add some film solvent to the jar and dissolve the scraps. Add only a little solvent at first and then add enough to make the solution "brushable." This solution keeps for months and can be thinned if necessary. The solution can be used for touching up a film stencil or in the making of a "reductive" stencil as described at the end of this chapter. I have also tried, with some success, using it instead of Maskoid in the "Maskoid and water-soluble filler" method. After the application of the thick liquid film solution and the water-soluble filler, the film is dissolved from the underside of the screen and the glue lifted off as well. The process is still in the experimental stage but shows promise.

Some limited special effects can be created on the film stencil before it adheres to the silk. Use a wood burning tool to burn away the lacquer rather than to cut it; with a fine, heated point, images can be burned into the film, or larger areas can be burned away with a blunt point.

2-41

2-41. PAT'S DREAM, 20 by 19¹/₂ inches, by Clifford
T. Chieffo, 1966. Medium: one color photographic
stencil printed on pewter-metallic paper. (Photograph
by Neal Hall.)

PHOTOGRAPHIC STENCILS

In recent years the photographic stencil has done more to bring the silk-screen process into the world of painting than any other stencil technique. Artists such as Robert Rauschenberg (Figure 2-42) and Andy Warhol (Figure 2-43) have already proved the aesthetic compatibility of the silk-screen process and painting. The photo stencil, in addition, has created a new interest for painters in silk-screen printmaking. Notable among these are: Roy Lichtenstein, Tom Wesselman, R. B. Kitaj (Figure 2-44), James Rosenquist, Robert Rauschenberg, Andy Warhol, Larry Rivers, and many others.

The characteristic ability of the photo stencil to reproduce a photographic image makes it a unique tool in printmaking and painting. In addition to this characteristic, it is one of the best means of printing the detail of a fine line drawing or a half-tone drawing with accuracy and sharpness.

The basic principle behind the photographic stencil process is simple. A chemically light-sensitive gelatin is placed either directly on the screen or on a temporary support of polyester film such as Mylar. A positive design rendered on a clear sheet of Mylar or a photographic positive is placed over the gelatin film and both are exposed to light. The light passing through the clear, non-opaque part of the design causes the gelatin to harden; the gelatin areas below the opaque areas of the design remain soft and are eventually washed away with water. Thus, that which was opaque in the original becomes an open area on the screen, and the rest becomes the blockout stencil.

There are two basic methods of creating a photographic stencil: one is the *direct* method, the other is the *transfer* method. In the direct method the screen itself is sensitized with a liquid solution, exposed, developed, and washed out so that the stencil is created directly on the screen. The transfer method involves the same steps as the direct method except that the photographic gelatin layer is sensitized, exposed, developed, etc., while on a temporary support of plastic. The gelatin film is then *transferred* to the screen, dried, and the plastic backing removed.

There are several variations of the methods just described, but it would be beyond the scope of this book to discuss all the possible techniques. For the artist's use, one stencil method belonging to the group of transfer film has been selected for description in these pages. This particular film and manufacturer were selected because the film requires less processing time than any other photo stencil material and is also designed to be used with inexpensive developers. The film is Type 4570 produced by the McGraw Colorgraph Company of Burbank, California,

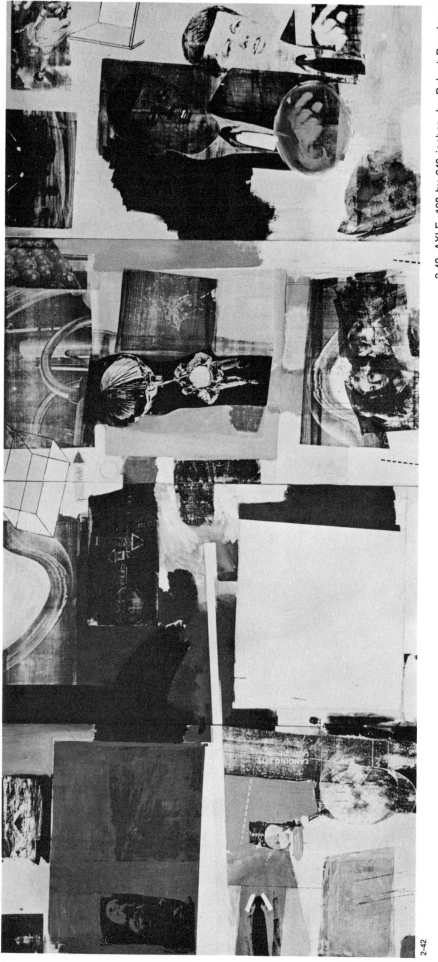

2-42. AXLE, 108 by 240 inches, by Robert Rauchenberg, 1964. Medium: oil on canvas with silk-screen stencils. Courtesy of the Leo Castelli Gallery, New York. (Photograph by Rudolph Burckhardt.)

2-42

2-43. JACKIE, 20 by 16 inches, by Andy Warhol, 1964. Medium: Acrylic silk-screen enamel on canvas. Courtesy of the Leo Castelli Gallery, New York. (Photograph by Rudolph Burckhardt.)

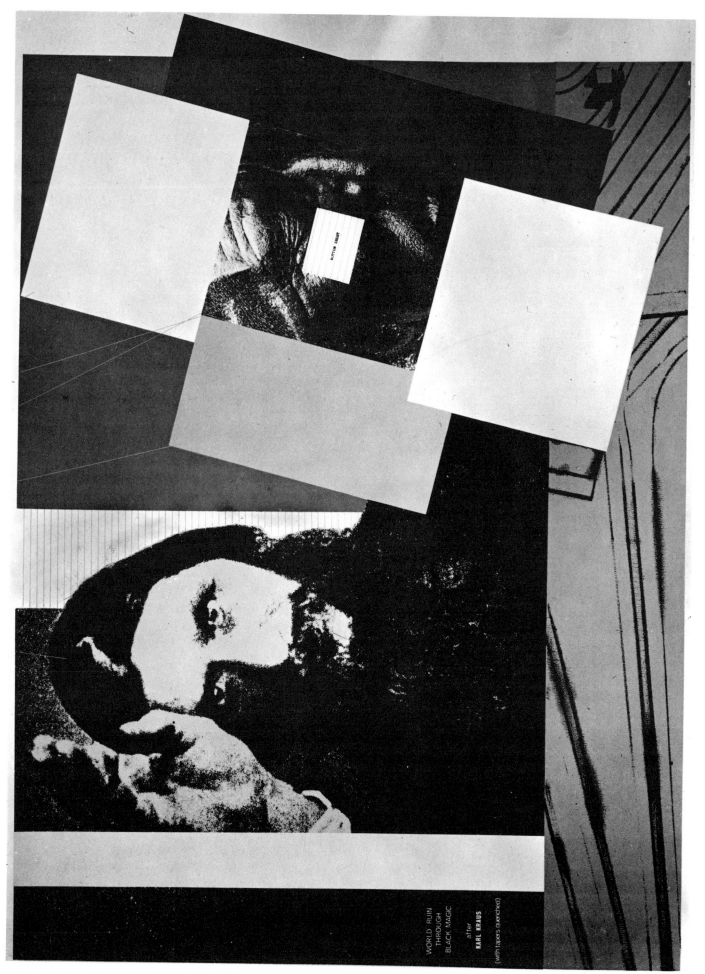

WORLD RUIN
THROUGH
BLACK MAGIC

after
KARL KRAUS

(with tapers quenched)

BEST-SUITED TECHNIQUES

EFFECTS DESIRED	Cut Film	Glue with Brush	Glue with Spray	Lacquer-Glue	Maskoid & Glue	Mimeograph Stencil	Paper Stencil	Photo Stencil Halftone Positive	Photo Stencil Hand-Drawn Positive	Tusche-Glue
Brushstroke		X		X	X			X	X	X
Straight line	X				X		X	X	X	
Curved line	X				X		X	X	X	
Cross-hatch				X	X		X	X	X	X
Soft edge			X				X	X		X
Graduated area		X			X			X		X
Reproduce a photograph								X		
Letters	X					X	X	X	X	
Typewritten letters						X		X		
Hard edge	X						X	X	X	
Textured look			X		X			X	X	X
Direct rubbing of texture						X				X
Splatter		X		X	X			X	X	X
Positive resist				X	X			X		
Negative resist		X								
Impasto							X			

2-44. Bottom half of WORLD RUIN THROUGH BLACK MAGIC, 54 by 38½ inches, by R. B. Kitaj, 1965. Medium: silk-screen print using photographic film stencils. Courtesy Marlborough-Gerson Gallery, New York. (Photograph by E. Nelson.)

one of the major suppliers of graphic art photographic materials. There are, of course, many companies that produce high quality photo stencil materials. The reader is encouraged to investigate various types and suppliers of films to discover equipment that will satisfy his specific needs.

The preparation of the art work or the photographic positive for the stencil involves two distinct processes.

1. Any image that is a photograph or wash drawing will contain half-tones or gradations of values between light and dark. In order to represent these half-tones in the finished stencil, the material must be photographed on a film that translates the grada-

73

2-45. Detail of PAT'S DREAM, 20 by 19½ inches, by Clifford T. Chieffo, 1966, showing dot patterns on a half-tone positive. (Photograph by Neal Hall.)

tions into a system of dot patterns (Figure 2-45). This negative is then printed onto a sensitized transparent backed film that renders the black dot pattern positive and opaque. Where there are no dots, the film remains transparent. This process is usually done by a photoengraver and the result is called a half-tone positive. The half-tone positive is now ready to be used to make the stencil for the silk-screen. The average half-tone positive for silk-screen work is generally photographed on an 85 line half-tone screen that is 85 black dots and white spaces per linear inch. The pictures used in Figure 2-41, "Pat's Dream," however, were photographed on a 133 line negative and then enlarged to two half-tone positives, one a 40-line positive and the other a 24-line positive. This was done so that the dot pattern became larger and more prominent and played a greater role in the total aesthetic configuration. The positives were then used to create the stencil which was attached to a number 16xx silk screen (a common mesh size for photo stencil work), and the edition was printed.

2. If the artist does not wish to use any half-tones or gradated values in his work, he can create his own transparent positive without a camera. Keeping in mind that the photo stencil is created by exposing parts of the stencil film to light and keeping the rest from the light, the artist can work directly on a sheet of acetate or other transparent film with a dense india ink, crayon, or any opaque material. The drawing may be in the form a fine opaque line, brush-strokes, drips, or a splash (Figure 2-46). Remember, regardless of the type of image used, it must in all cases be *opaque*. When the photo stencil is complete, all the areas that were opaque on the positive will be open so that you can print with any color and any type screen process paint.

Once the positive is complete, you may use the following directions which are a combination of my notes and a condensation of the processing instructions of McGraw Colorgraph's Type 4570 film to create the stencil for the silk-screen. The chemicals and exposure times are specific, but the order and the process are general enough to apply to most sheet film.

49/50   Adolph Gottlieb 1966

2-46

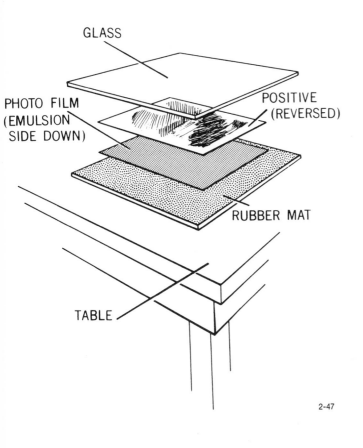

GLASS

PHOTO FILM
(EMULSION
SIDE DOWN)

POSITIVE
(REVERSED)

RUBBER MAT

TABLE

2-47

Step 1 — Handling the Film

Unwrap, handle, and process this film under dim tungsten or yellow "safe" light. A yellow "Bug Bulb" will be useful if a photographic "safe" light is not available. Always keep the unused film stored in a cool, dark place.

Step 2 — Exposing the Film

During the exposure of the film to light, close contact between the photographic positive and the film is necessary. A photographic contact printing frame is sold for this purpose but it is expensive. A simple version can be made by placing a thin rubber or foam mat on a plate of glass or smooth table top. Then lay the film with the shiny emulsion side down on the glass, with the positive placed on top of the film. Finally, sandwich everything together with a sheet of plate glass. The weight of the top glass will generally hold the film and positive in good contact (Figure 2-47).

Be sure that the film is exposed *through* the plastic backing or *dull* side of the photo stencil. This also means that the left and right hand sides of the positive will be reversed when the film is adhered to the screen. Therefore any lettering should appear "wrong reading" during exposure.

A single light source should be used for obtaining the sharpest detail. A 35 amp carbon arc 60 inches from the film will produce a normal stencil in 4 minutes. A General Electric "Sunlamp" may also be used at closer distances. An average stencil 12 to 14 inches square exposed with a G.E. Sunlamp at a 20-inch distance from the film will take about 2 minutes (Figure 2-48). The exact exposure time can be determined by the following test.

A. Cut a small piece of film, say 4 by 6 inches and place it beneath the positive under an area that is representative of the total positive.
B. Cover the entire film area with four strips of cardboard.
C. Place the G.E. Sunlamp 20 inches away and prepare to time the exposure.
D. Mark the cardboard strips 1, 2, 3, and 4 minutes, turn on the light and remove strip #4. One minute later remove strip #3; after one more minute remove strip #2, etc. At the end of 4 minutes turn the light off, develop, wash-out the film and let it dry.

2-46. RED HALO-WHITE GROUND, 24 by 18 inches, by Adolph Gottlieb, 1966. Medium: silk-screen. Courtesy of the Marlborough-Gerson Gallery, New York. (Photograph by Clifford T. Chieffo.)

2-48

2-49

You will notice that at one end of the sheet the gelatin film will be thin and at the other end thick. In the thicker portion, the side exposed to the most light, the detail may be lost and a thin film may be covering the open areas. This means that part of the gelatin film is overexposed. You can then determine the correct exposure time by observing the test strip that yields the sharpest detail.

This test sheet should be saved so that you can identify a possible exposure problem in your next stencil. Remember, more light creates a thicker stencil and may block out detail; less light creates a thinner stencil.

For larger size films the distance should be increased between the bulb and top glass proportionately and the exposure time should be squared when the bulb-to-glass distance is doubled. Experiment to determine the correct exposure time.

2-50

Step 3 — Developing the film
The film should be developed for 2 minutes in a 2 percent potassium dichromate solution ($2\frac{1}{2}$ ounces by weight per gallon of water) or $\frac{1}{2}$ percent solution of hydrogen peroxide in water. The film may be developed in a tray (Figure 2-49) or it may be placed on a flat, level surface, emulsion side up, and a small quantity of solution poured on and spread to wet the emulsion completely. Rubber gloves should be worn to protect the artist's hands. The developing process should be done under the yellow "safe" light.

Step 4 — Washing Out the Unexposed Areas
Flood the film with warm water (115°–125°F), until all the gelatin that was not exposed to light is removed (Figure 2-50). It takes about 1 minute for the image to appear as the unexposed gelatin melts and is washed away. Continue washing for 1 minute after the image seems to be completely clear in all open areas. Chill with *very* cold water or rinse the film several times with a 50 percent alcohol solution. The use of alcohol shortens the drying time and helps keep fine detail open.

2-51

Step 5 — Attaching the Film to the Screen
Place the wet, washed-out film emulsion side up, on a flat, level, absorbent support. The support should be no larger than the format area of the silk and for best contact should not extend under the wood frame. A towel can be stretched over the support to provide the absorbency (Figure 2-51).

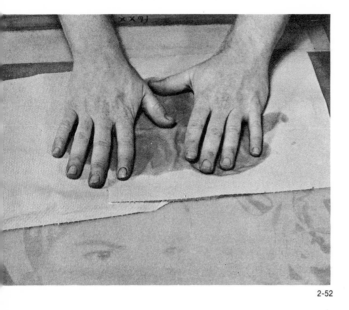

2-52

Carefully position the screen over the stencil and gently lower into contact. Lightly blot the excess moisture from the top of the screen with several sheets of paper towels or clean unprinted newsprint (Figure 2-52). *DO NOT ROLL WITH A BRAYER* (ROLLER). Do not press the screen too hard against the film or it will distort the image. Weight the frame and leave undisturbed for 10 minutes. A fan may be used to hasten drying, but do not use warm air until the very end of the drying period.

When thoroughly dry, after about 1 hour, the plastic film base can be peeled off If the plastic base is difficult to remove, the film is not completely dry. Block out the area beyond the stencil with glue, lacquer, or a paper mask. The stencil is now ready for printing.

Before beginning to make the stencil the artist should check the following points.

A. Make sure that the opaque areas on the positive are completely opaque and that the transparent areas are clean and free from dust.
B. Be sure that the top glass is clean and free from dust.
C. New (previously unused) stretched fabrics of natural silk, Nylon, polyester (Dacron, etc.) or stainless steel should always be scrubbed with trisodium phosphate and rinsed thoroughly with hot water just before the screen is applied to a stencil.

2-53

Step 6 — Removing the Stencil after Printing
When using Colorgraph's Stencil Remover, follow these directions taken from the label on the container. Thoroughly clean the screen, and remove the paint with the appropriate solvent. Wet the stencil with hot water on both sides to swell and warm the gelatin. (Trisodium phosphate may help in this operation since it degreases the stencil, which can therefore become wet and swell more readily.) Place the screen stencil side down, on a flat surface and sprinkle the stencil remover sparingly over the screen (Figure 2-53). With a clean cloth, wet with warm water (90°–105°F), and spread the remover evenly over the stencil area (Figure 2-54).

2-54

It is not necessary to dissolve the stencil completely. As soon as enough gelatin has been dissolved to break the bond with the silk, the stencil may be washed off with hot water and scrubbed with a clean brush if necessary (Figure 2-55). Mark this brush and reserve it for "ENZYME ONLY."

Neutralize any possible traces of Stencil Remover (enzyme) with 1 ounce per gallon muriatic (hydrochloric) acid. Be sure to neutralize the screen frame as well as the fabric. Rinse very thoroughly. Scrub the wet screen with a clean brush marked "FOR TSP ONLY" with trisodium phosphate, and follow by a thorough rinsing with hot water. The two most important points to remember are: One, enzyme Stencil Remover must be neutralized, or the next stencil will be attacked and weakened or destroyed. Two, the last operation before a new stencil is applied must always be a degreasing with trisodium phosphate (Oakite) only (*not* proprietary cleaners containing detergents and wetting agents such as Ajax, etc.).

Another important point to keep in mind is that the bond of gelatin stencils to natural silk and to stainless steel is fundamentally good, provided that these materials have been properly cleaned and degreased with TSP. The bond of gelatin stencils (any) to Nylon and Polyester fabrics is superficial and inadequate regardless of cleaning techniques. The surface of these man-made fibers must undergo a molecular change before true adhesion can be established with the stencil.

The McGraw Colorgraph Company has developed treatment to accomplish this conversion. For Nylon they have developed their "Nylon Surface Converting Fluid," and for polyester (Dacron, Teritol, etc.) they have "McGraw's Polyester Bonding Acid."

For a more complete analysis and description of other photo stencil techniques, the reader is referred to two excellent source books on the subject: *Techniques in Photography for the Silk Screen Printer* by Robert O. Fossett, and *Photographic Screen Process Printing* by Albert Kosloff.

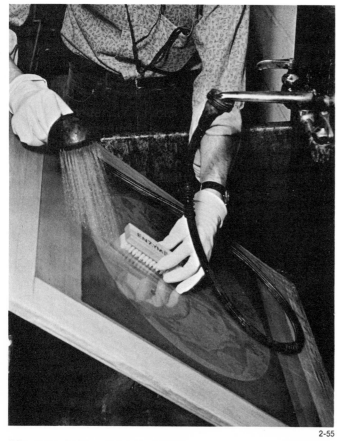

2-55

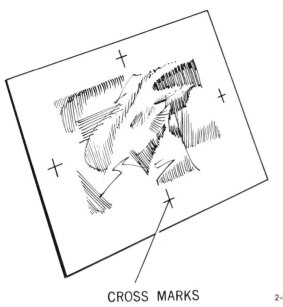

CROSS MARKS   2-56

STENCIL 1

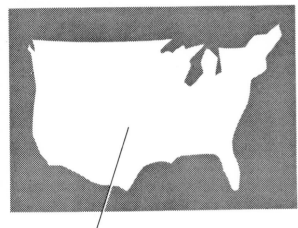

ENTIRE SHAPE PRINTED YELLOW   2-57

STENCIL 2

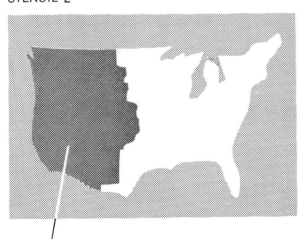

SHAPE THAT IS TO REMAIN YELLOW
IS BLOCKED OUT   2-58

Three final additions to this chapter need mentioning here.

1. When film stencils are used in multicolor printing, the following registration method may aid you in achieving proper registration for each color. On the master-sketch four cross marks are drawn in the margin, one in the middle of each side (Figure 2-56). The film stencil is then cut or processed (photo) with the cross marks included as part of the open areas of the stencil. Next, the master-sketch is registered in the register tabs on the baseboard and the film stencil registered so that the cross marks match; the screen is then lowered and finally the film adheres to the screen while it is still in position on the baseboard. This process is followed for each color stencil.

Once the stencil is intact on the screen, the cross marks are printed on each sheet. If the registration is not correct on any sheet, it will immediately show up at the cross marks. The cross marks are later cut off from the margin of the finished print. When the margin is not large enough to permit any cutting, the cross marks are printed only on the first few proofs and then blocked out on the stencil with tape, paper, glue, or lacquer for the printing of the remainder of the edition. For each new stencil these registration proofs are printed first. If they fail to coincide with the printed cross marks of the last stencil, the registration tabs may have to be adjusted.

2. Often it is necessary to print five or six small color shapes in a relatively condensed area of a large screen. Rather than using tusche or Maskoid to make a positive of first one color and then the next, and glueing and washing out the screen after each color, the artist will probably find it easier to use what I call a *reductive stencil*.

The process begins by making a simple negative blockout stencil using glue, water-soluble filler, lacquer, or paper that follows the shape of the outlines of all the separate color areas (Figure 2-57). The first color is printed through this entire open area. Print the lightest opaque colors first or if transparent colors are to be used, print them first unless you plan to utilize transparent colors later to create two or more colors by using an overlaying stencil relationship as described on page 84. After the first color stencil is printed, assume for example the color is light yellow, the area that is to remain light yellow in the finished print is blocked out on the second stencil. This is accomplished by adding more blockout filler to the stencil (Figure 2-58). The second color is then printed through all of the remaining open area and after printing, the shape the artist desires for that color is blocked out. This process of reducing the size of the open area with each stencil is continued until the last color shape is printed.

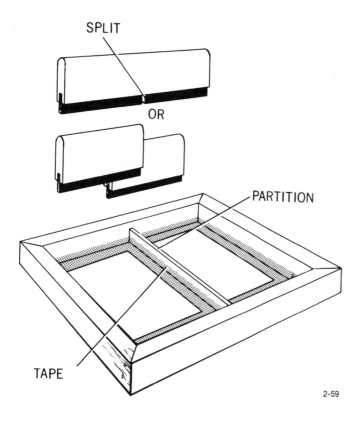

SPLIT

OR

PARTITION

TAPE

2-59

This process is interesting because the final shape of the color area is defined not by the stencil used to print that color, but by the stencil and overprinting of the next color. Thus it is like defining a figure by painting in the negative space or the background around the figure.

In my practice, I have found that the solution made from scraps of lacquer film (Nu-Film, Pro Film, etc.) and solvent (page 67) makes an excellent, quick drying, blockout medium for these small areas. In the cleaning process, after the paint has been removed, the lacquer film solution can readily be dissolved by a light rubbing with a rag soaked with its solvent.

3. *Split Screen Printing* is a way of printing two colors simultaneously on the same screen. If the two colors to be printed are separated by no less than 1 inch, they can be successfully printed by building a partition of thin wood or cardboard between the open stencil areas. The wood or cardboard is taped to the inside of the screen and the respective color is poured into its half of the screen. Two small squeegees, one for each color, are then used to print each color before the screen is lifted. One large squeegee can be used if a slice of rubber is removed from the blade so that the blade will pass over the partition and two colors printed in one stroke. In this case, the partition must be lower than the height of the rubber squeegee blade to insure good printing contact with the silk (Figure 2-59).

3. Making a Print

MASTER-SKETCH INTERPRETATION

The master-sketch for creating a sik-screen print may be as simple as a rough draft with color indications or as complicated as a completed painting. Since every artist has his own particular inclinations and attitudes towards a working master-plan, it is rather difficult to be dogmatic or insistent upon a specific type of sketch for producing a silk-screen print.

Silk-screen printing, like sculpture, requires that the artist work with separate parts or on different portions of the work of art. He can only observe his work as a total entity when the parts are complete. This, of course, happens in painting also, but the time difference between the beginning and the finished product is not as great a conscious factor as it is in silk-screen printing.

In addition, there are several mechanical steps which must be performed during printing which may interrupt the creative flow. Of course, most silk-screen artists regard these steps not as deterents but as crucial elements of the craft and productive sources in image formulation. In any case, it is generally advisable to work from some sort of master-sketch or some concept of the complete image.

The use of a master-sketch does not preclude deviating from it to make allowances or enhancements determined by the media. I have seen some artists work slavishly close to a completed painting used as a master-plan, and other artists who have worked without any plan whatsoever — i.e., the next stencil was determined organically from the one just printed. In both cases the results were magnificent. The master-sketch, when used as an exact source in the stencil-making process, should be made on the same size and type paper as the printing stock.

In analyzing the different stencils to be made, I have found it generally advisable to print the largest areas first and the fine details last. Likewise it is advisable, as in the glaze technique in painting, to build the color from the lighter tones to the darker. The silk-screen medium allows for a great deal of flexibility in

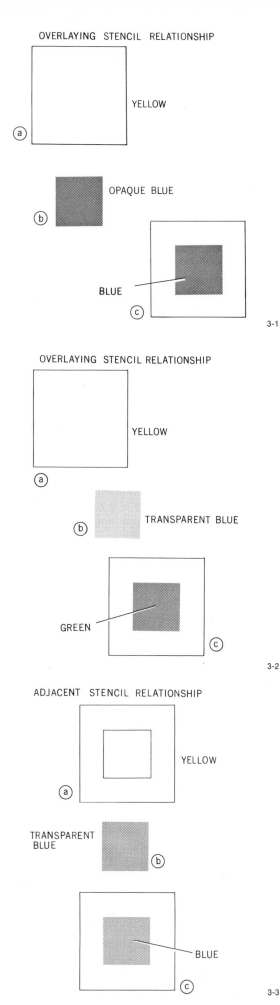

OVERLAYING STENCIL RELATIONSHIP

YELLOW

(a)

OPAQUE BLUE

(b)

BLUE

(c)

3-1

OVERLAYING STENCIL RELATIONSHIP

YELLOW

(a)

TRANSPARENT BLUE

(b)

GREEN

(c)

3-2

ADJACENT STENCIL RELATIONSHIP

YELLOW

(a)

TRANSPARENT BLUE

(b)

BLUE

(c)

3-3

deciding stencil sequence. Color effects may be created by working from transparent to opaque color or just the reverse — dark colors may be printed first and overlayed with lighter colors. Therefore, the artist should not be overly preoccupied with stencil sequence. In fact, if you are a painter, you may generally proceed with your usual sequence in building your image. The stencil analysis experience you gain in making your first print will far surpass anything that I might write in these brief paragraphs.

BASIC FACTORS IN MULTICOLOR PRINTING

Once you have determined the amount and sequence of the color stencils to be used, there are a few basic factors in multicolor printing and stencil relationships that bear mention here. These factors of stencil relationships are meant to reduce the problems of multiregistrations and possibly to be a functioning element in the final image.

The opaqueness or transparency of a color may dictate its sequence in printing and/or the type of stencil relationship used for its printing. Let us assume we want to print a small dark blue square in the center of a larger yellow square. If the smaller blue square is an opaque blue the problem is simple. The yellow square is printed in its entirety with one stencil (Figure 3-1A). The smaller, opaque blue stencil (Figure 3-1B) is then superimposed in the center of the yellow square (Figure 3-1C). The blue, being opaque, will cover the yellow beneath it and the desired effect will be achieved. If, however, the small blue square is transparent, using the above process would yield a green square in the center of the yellow square (Figures 3-2A, B, and C) — with the transparent blue appearing green when printed on the yellow background. Thus, in order to print a transparent blue square in the center of a larger yellow square, a different stencil relationship must be used. The yellow square would have to be printed with its center left blank (Figure 3-3A), and the transparent blue square (Figure 3-3B) printed in the blank area. In this way a blue square will appear in the center of the larger yellow square (Figure 3-2C).

Our discussion of transparency and opaqueness of colors has also involved two of the major stencil relationships. In Figures 3-1C and 3-2C, a superimposing or overlaying relationship is in effect, and in Figure 3-3C there is an adjacent or side-by-side relationship. The latter of the two relationships is the most difficult to align. In most cases in an adjacent stencil relationship where an opaque color is used as the top color, it can slightly overlap the bottom color's edge by 1/16 of an inch. In this way the align-

Artists proof for Love, Marriage, Business   *Chieffo '66*

C-11. LOVE, MARRIAGE, BUSINESS, 24 by 22 inches, by Clifford T. Chieffo, 1966. Medium: silk-screen on brown, all-purpose paper. (Photograph by Neal Hall.)

OVERLAPPING STENCIL RELATIONSHIP

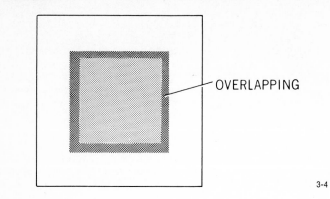

—OVERLAPPING

3-4

ment and printing process will be less critical. (See Figure 3-4.) This technique of overlapping the edge of the color below can be used to good advantage in creating a third color and *shape* if a transparent color is used as the overlapping stencil (Figure 3-5A, B, and C). Thus, through careful planning, you can use fewer stencils without sacrificing color or image, and the effects of compound stencils can be multiplied.

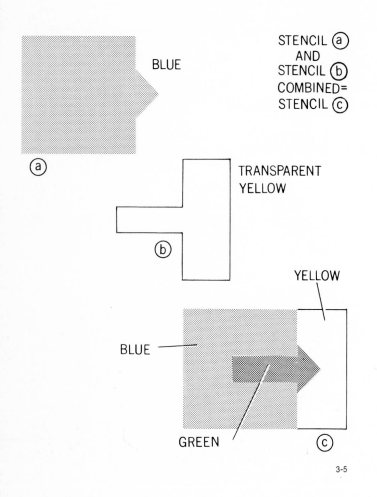

BLUE

STENCIL ⓐ
AND
STENCIL ⓑ
COMBINED=
STENCIL ⓒ

ⓐ

TRANSPARENT
YELLOW

ⓑ

YELLOW

BLUE

GREEN

ⓒ

3-5

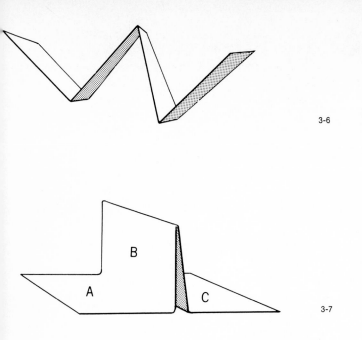

3-6

REGISTRATION

To maintain accurate alignment of the stock during the printing process, register tabs or blocks should be used. The register tab is used for printing most papers and the block type is used for printing thicker stock; i.e., cardboard, glass, plastic, etc.

Register tabs can easily be made from a slightly stiff paper or paper gummed tape. In either case, the paper or tape is cut into a strip approximately $1/2$ inch by 2 inches. This strip is then folded in half with both halves then folded back to the center fold (Figure 3-6), creating an accordion-type fold. The ends (A and C) are flattened out and pushed together toward the center (B) (Figure 3-7).

To affix the tabs to the baseboard, the master-sketch is first aligned under the screen and taped down (Figure 3-8). One half of the tab is fitted under the

3-7

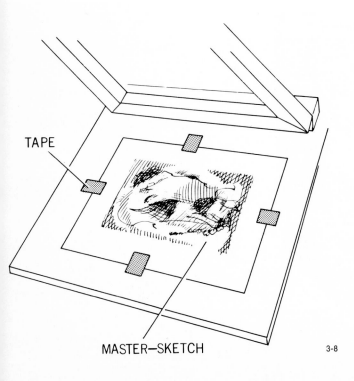

TAPE

MASTER—SKETCH

3-8

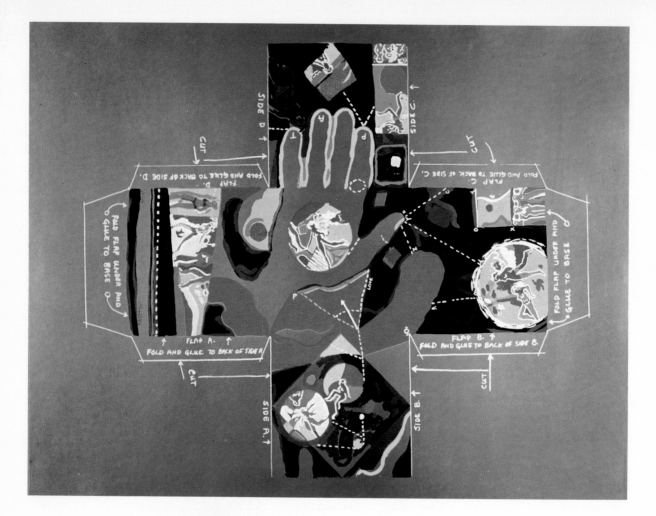

C-12. IN THE BEGINNING, 26 by 20 inches, by Clifford T. Chieffo, 1966. Medium: silk-screen on pewter-metallic paper. (Photograph by Neal Hall.)

C-13. IN THE BEGINNING, 6-inch cube, by Clifford T. Chieffo. Medium: silk-screen on folded pewter-metallic paper. (Photograph by Neal Hall.)

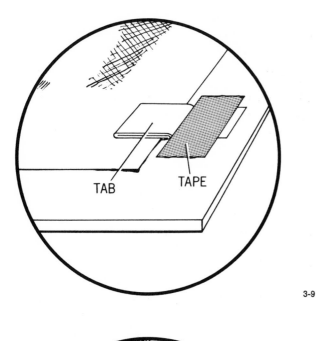

3-9

sketch. The center portion of the tab is folded snugly over the sketch and held while the remaining half is taped to the baseboard (Figure 3-9). The corner of the sketch is then lifted and the remaining end of the tab is taped down (Figure 3-10). When using the gummed tape tab, you can eliminate taping. Moisten the tab and glue it into place. Three tabs are generally used for registration: two on the bottom or top of the sketch and one on either the right or left side (Figure 3-11). The folding tab also functions to hold the paper in place during printing once the screen has been lowered.

TAB TAPE

TAB

TAPE

3-10

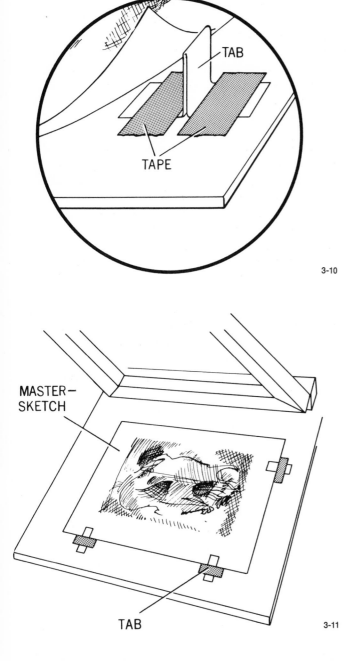

MASTER—SKETCH

TAB

3-11

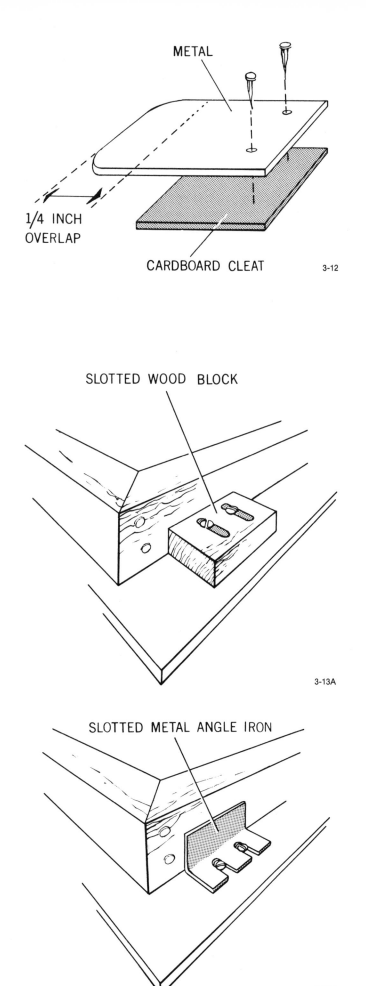

METAL

1/4 INCH OVERLAP

CARDBOARD CLEAT

3-12

SLOTTED WOOD BLOCK

3-13A

SLOTTED METAL ANGLE IRON

3-13B

When printing heavy stock a version of the tab called the block made from cardboard and tin or aluminum may be used. These blocks must be placed beyond the edge of the screen frame or they will prevent the screen from making good printing contact with the baseboard. The block is constructed from tin, aluminum, or heavy acetate and a piece of cardboard cut from the printing stock. These pieces are nailed together directly onto the baseboard in position for good registration (Figure 3-12). The metal acts as the flap and the cardboard as the stop or cleat.

The cardboard can be used alone as a cleat when you are sure that the stock will not slide upward and over it. Sliding is generally not a problem when heavy, thick stock is being printed on. If a more substantial cleat is called for, a flat iron brace screwed to the baseboard may be used.

Occasionally a misregistration may occur in spite of the fact that the stock is aligned properly in the guides. There are several factors that may contribute to this problem. One factor is that if the silk is too loose, it may "roll" in front of the squeegee during printing. When the silk is loose, but not loose enough to require restretching, you can use products designed to shrink the silk taut after they are applied to the silk that is close to the border of the frame.

Another factor that may cause misregistration is a loose hinge. Always check the hinge screws for looseness before printing. If the screws are tight and the hinge connection is still loose, the hingepin can be removed and bent *slightly* with a hammer and then re-engaged to tighten the connection. If, in the case of a larger screen, the problem still persists, it may be necessary to use adjustable alignment blocks. The blocks are made from slotted wood or metal angle iron and screwed to the baseboard, one on each side of the printing frame. These blocks will provide a snug hold for the free end of the screen during printing (Figures 3-13A and B). Slots cut into the blocks make them adjustable to slightly different size screens and screens that have swelled after washing with water.

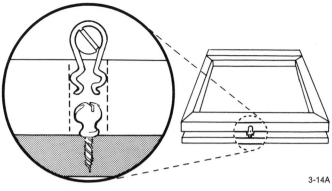

3-14A

Two other devices that may be used for alignment are a friction-type snap catch (Figure 3-14A), and a peg and hole arrangement (Figure 3-14B). When alignment blocks are used, the printing stock must always be the same size as the overall size of the screen frame or smaller.

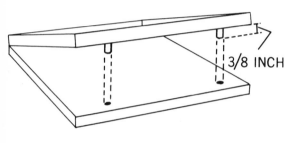

3/8 INCH

3-14B

STEP-BY-STEP PROCEDURE FOR PRINTING WITH THE MASKOID METHOD

This portion of the chapter will deal with a brief step-by-step description of the silk-screen process using the Maskoid method.

3-15

3-16

Step 1 — Quantity of Paper
Once the type of paper or printing stock has been selected, a decision must be made as to how many prints will be in the edition. In addition to this total number, several more sheets of paper, say 10 percent of the total, should be added to allow for sheets that will have to be removed from the final edition because of misprints, stencil or color changes, or damage due to mishandling. Additional sheets of paper are to be added if single and progressive proofs are to be taken during printing.

A single proof is a print of each stencil or color printed on a separate sheet of paper. These single proofs are useful if later it should become necessary to duplicate a particular stencil in the series.

A progressive proof is a print of each color or stencil combined with the preceding stencils. The first progressive proof would be a combination of stencil one and two. The second progressive proof is a combination of stencils one and two plus the third, etc. Progressive proofs serve as a good record for learning the effect of certain colors, textures, areas, etc., on the total image. It also makes a valuable teaching aid when the process is demonstrated to another artist or students.

Step 2 — Preparing the Stencil
The Maskoid is applied to the screen according to the effects desired (See Maskoid, Chapter 2, page 50), and allowed to dry (Figure 3-15).

Step 3 — Applying the Filler
Apply the water-soluble prepared filler or glue in the following manner:
  A. Cut a piece of cardboard or mat board 3 by 5 inches with a straight, sharp edge to use as a squeegee for the filler.
  B. Pour a small amount of filler on one of the taped border areas, never directly on the open printing area. LePage's Strength Glue may be thinned with water in a one to one ratio (Figure 3-16).

3-17

3-18

3-19

C. Squeegee the glue across the screen, Maskoid areas included, with the stiff piece of cardboard (Figure 3-17). When the first coating is complete, scoop up the remaining excess glue and allow the screen to dry. When dry, apply a second coat if necessary.

Always apply the filler to the *top side* of the screen only. If any filler should seep through the mesh to the silk side, it should be carefully wiped away. Check for pinholes or any "skipped" areas by holding the screen up against a light or window. Touch up any pinholes with a small brush. Allow the screen to dry.

Step 4 — Preparing the Paint
The paint should be thinned to the consistency of heavy cream. Consult Chapter 5 on paints for recommended use of varnishes, transparent filler base, mineral spirits, etc. The paint may be mixed on a small glass palette or in jars or cans.

Step 5 — Removing the Maskoid
Remove the Maskoid areas by rubbing with a square of natural rubber (Figure 3-18). See Chapter 2, page 55 for details of Maskoid removal. Check to see if all former Maskoid areas are now open and clear.

Step 6 — Ready for Printing
Check all mechanical operations of the screen, including hinges, hingebar, prop bars, etc., and the drying facilities. Be sure that there are no nicks or cuts in the squeegee blade and that it is clean and sharp.

Step 7 — Registration
Register a piece of extra stock under the screen (Figure 3-19). This sheet will serve as a color tester and will allow the artist to see and examine the results of the particular applied stencil technique in addition to seeing if any paint is printing in an unwanted area. If there are pinholes in the stencil filler through which the paint is printing, they may be blocked up with a thin piece of paper held in place with transparent tape. The tape alone may be used when small editions are printed. If extensive areas are at fault, clear the screen of paint with paint thinner, dry and touch up the spots with the original filler.

3-20

3-21

Step 8 — Printing
Pour a liberal amount of paint at one end of the screen (Figure 3-20). Enough paint should be used to print eight to twelve sheets before the supply is replenished. Of course, the number of sheets able to be printed will depend partly on how open the stencil is, the consistency of paint, the pressure on the squeegee, the absorbency of the stock, etc. The amount of paint carried across the screen with the squeegee does not dictate the amount of paint deposited or the thickness of the printed layer. It is better to have a little too much paint in reserve than to run dry during a squeegee stroke. After you have poured in the paint, grasp the squeegee firmly and, depending on the type squeegee you have, draw or push it across the screen (Figures 1-27 and 1-28).

Step 9 — Removal of Stock
After one stroke has been completed, lift the screen and remove the stock (Figure 3-21). If the stock should adhere to the silk, the paint may be too thick. It can be thinned with a varnish prepared for that purpose, or with a small amount of mineral spirits. This type of adhesion is a common problem that generally disappears after the first one or two sheets of stock have been printed. It generally will not interfere with the quality of the print.

If you are using a transparent color you may wish to use two strokes of the squeegee across the screen to intensify the color. The two strokes of an opaque color, however, will not show any appreciable difference in the final color. You should be aware of the fact, however, that the second stroke generally will produce a slightly blurred edge which may or may not be desirable.

Step 10 — Registration of Second Sheet
When the first sheet has been removed from the baseboard and placed to dry, register a second sheet, lower the screen and repeat the printing process. The run is complete for that stencil when all the sheets are printed including single proofs, progressive proofs, and the regular edition series.

3-22

3-23

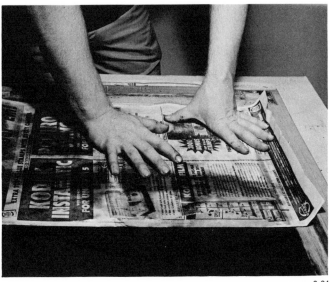

3-24

Step 11 — Paint Clean-up

There are many methods of cleaning the paint from the screen, and the following is just one procedure that works effectively.

Remove the bulk of the excess paint by scraping it into one corner of the screen with a piece of cardboard. A piece of cardboard folded into a "V" shape or two pieces, one in each hand, can be used to scoop the excess paint into a jar or can (Figure 3-22). Several sheets of newspapers are then placed beneath the screen. The screen can remain on the baseboard, or if space permits, moved to another area. A liberal amount of mineral spirits or varsol is then poured on the top side of the screen and spread to all corners with a large rag or paper towels (Figure 3-23). Next, spread a sheet of newspaper on top of the screen to remove most of the paint (Figure 3-24). This procedure is repeated until most of the paint is removed. The top sheets of newspaper beneath the screen should be removed as soon as they are soaked with the paint and mineral spirits.

The screen is finally propped up or placed carefully in a wood vise and rubbed simultaneously on both sides with rags soaked in paint solvent (mineral spirits). Rub the screen with dry rags and allow it to stand until all traces of the solvent are gone.

When the screen has thoroughly dried, check for any paint that may still be clogging the mesh. Try to remove these traces with the thinner or solvent, and if they fail, resort to acetone or *liquid* brush cleaner. If the mesh is clear, but a color stain is present on the fabric, the acetone or brush cleaner will generally remove it. Although some staining is expected, it should be removed when it interferes visually with the next stencil application. To complete the operation, thoroughly clean the squeegee, palette, and any other tools used during the printing.

Step 12 — Glue or Water-Soluble Filler Removal

If a prepared water-soluble filler has been used, check the directions on the label to see if you should use warm or cool water for its removal. Glue can be removed with warm water. The screen is placed in a tub or sink and the filler removed with a pressured stream of water. Scrub any stubborn areas of glue gently with a small hand brush. If a tub or sink is not available the procedure described for the removal of paint may be used with, of course, *water* as the solvent.

Step 13 — Separating the Proofs

When all the stencils have been run and the prints dry, the single and progressive proofs should be labeled and removed from the group. The remaining group should be examined for consistency and faults.

Prints that do not meet the standards of the artist should be destroyed. There are some cases, however, when the quality of a particular single print is high, but because of a color or stencil change, these prints do not match the bulk of the series or edition. These unique, one-of-a-kind prints should be labeled "artist's proof" number one, two, three, etc. After the various proofs have been removed from the main group, the remaining number should be counted and numbered in sequence.

There are two existing schools of thought on whether or not silk-screen prints should be sequentially numbered and whether the signature should appear in the print area, included in a stencil or signed in pencil below the printed area.

The school against sequential numbering maintains that unlike the arts of lithography and etching, there is no appreciable difference between the first print and the last; therefore sequential numbering is superfluous. I am in agreement with the second school of thought, namely that which proposes the use of sequential numbering and a pencil signature. The justification for the use of numbers is their use in keeping records of the edition. The records may serve to supply information on the whereabouts of specific prints in the edition, prizes and exhibition history of each print, etc.

In any case, the difference between numbering or not is of little consequence. If, however, you wish to number your prints, the following system should be used. Two numbers are involved — the first is the number of the particular print, the second is the total number of prints in the edition. The two numbers placed in the lower left-hand corner generally appear as a fraction or are separated by a hyphen. For example, the numbers 6/50 would mean that this print is the sixth in a total edition of fifty. The pencil signature should appear in the lower right-hand corner.

REPAIRS

Torn Silk
Occasionally through mishandling or by accident, a small rip may occur in the silk. If the rip occurs during the printing operation and in the border area of the screen, it can temporarily be sealed with a piece of masking tape on each side of the screen until the edition is completed. Later, the masking tape can be removed and replaced with bits of paper or gummed-paper tape applied to both sides of the screen and sealed with lacquer or shellac. Small punctures in the image area can be left untouched as they will not interfere with the passage of paint or the quality of the print. Other small punctures in the border area should be sealed with a drop of lacquer or shellac.

Once the screen material begins to develop runs and tears in normal use, it is generally an indication that the material is wearing out and will soon need replacement.

Torn Tape Border
The gummed-paper tape border occasionally tears or lifts up during printing. When this occurs, a piece of masking tape should immediately be applied to the damaged area to prevent the paint from leaking through the screen. Next, the screen should be thoroughly cleaned of paint and dried. The old, torn tape, along with the masking tape should be removed and replaced with new tape and then resealed with shellac as described in "Taping and Sealing" (page 22).

TABLE OF SOLVENTS

Material	To Thin	To Remove
Dried pigment		Acetone, liquid brush cleaner
Enamel paint	Mineral spirits, turpentine	Mineral spirits, turpentine, kerosene
Glue	Water	Water
Lacquer filler	Lacquer thinner	Laquer thinner
Lacquer films		Lacquer thinner, destenciling solvent
Lacquer paints	Lacquer thinner	Lacquer thinner
Lithograph crayon		Turpentine
Maskoid	Soapy water	Rub off, mineral spirits
Oil-based paint	Turpentine, mineral spirits	Mineral spirits, turpentine, kerosene
Shellac	Alcohol	Alcohol
Tempera paint	Water	Water
Tusche liquid or stick	Water	Mineral spirits, turpentine, kerosene
WaterSol	One part methyl alcohol and two parts ethylene dichloride*	Cool water
Wax crayon		Turpentine, mineral spirits, kerosene

*Ethylene dichloride is also used as a plastics adhesive and can generally be obtained at a plastics supply house.

4. Printing Papers and Printing on Canvas

PRINTING PAPERS

Almost any paper of good quality will be suitable for silk-screen printing. Printing and handling is easier if the paper is slightly heavier, but lightweight papers can be used if they are kept flat during the entire working process. Certainly, the larger the sheet of paper is the heavier it should be. The paper should be fairly absorbent, although not so absorbent that it draws the oils from the paint which cause a ring to form around the color and the structure of the paint film to be weakened.

One hundred percent rag content paper is probably the best to use because of its durability and non-yellowing characteristics, but 100 percent or even 50 percent rag content papers are very expensive. I have found that inexpensive, smooth watercolor paper with a 140 pound weight (the weight of the sheet denoted by the weight of 500 sheets or one ream), and two ply Bristol Board or Bainbridge Board satisfactory. Good quality index paper is readily available and makes an excellent printing stock.

The variety of textures and colors and sizes available in papers are too numerous to mention. Suffice it to say that selecting paper is largely a matter of personal choice. It should be noted however, that textured paper and colored paper, such as the Degas All-Purpose Paper used in the print on page 85, will have a definite effect on the printed color. Transparent colors are more susceptible to texture, as noted in the section on "impasto" printing (page 59), and to colored paper. Metallic papers in silver, pewter or gold produce a metallic, luminous effect on transparent colors. Even charcoal paper may be used (Figure 4-1), but admittedly the thinness of this paper makes handling difficult; too much bending or flexing may cause the paint to crack. Buying paper from a wholesale house in 100 sheet lots can bring the cost of printing down considerably.

As noted in the Preface, once the stencil is affixed to the screen, any reasonably smooth surface can be used for printing — Plexiglas, metal, glass, wood, fabric, cardboard, and canvas — provided that the proper type of paint in each case is employed.

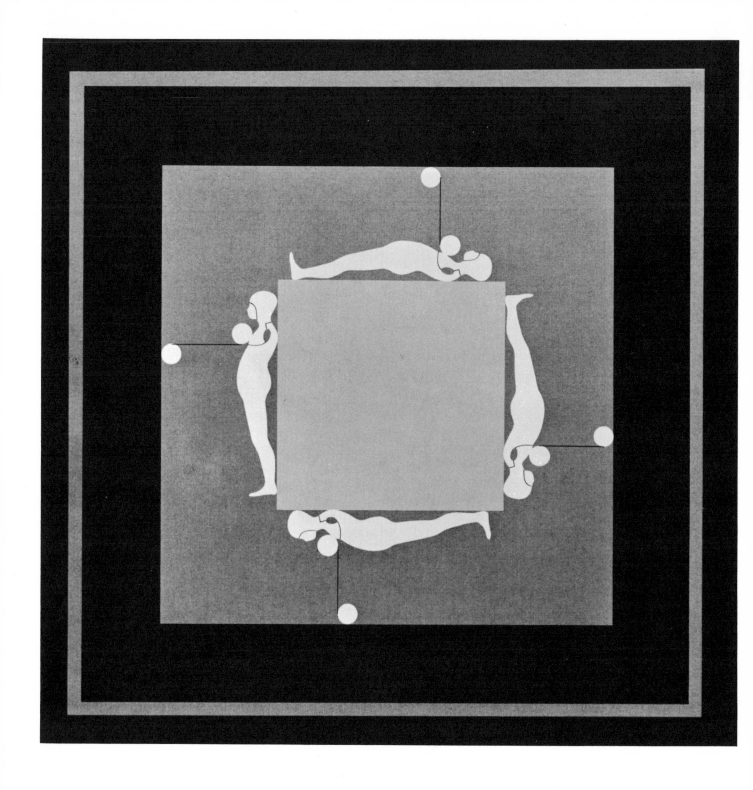

4-1. FOUR FIGURES AROUND THE SQUARE, 26 by 26 inches, by Ernest T. Trova, 1965. Medium: silkscreen on beige paper. Collection of the author. (Photograph by Neal Hall.)

4-2. Detail of AXLE, 108 by 240 inches, by Robert Rauchenberg, 1964, showing the combination of silkscreen photographic stencil with direct painting. Courtesy of the Leo Castelli Gallery, New York. (Original photograph by Rudolph Burckhardt; detail photograph by Neal Hall.)

PRINTING ON CANVAS

Printing on canvas, either stretched or unstretched, is a simple matter (Figure 4-2). The canvas should have a relatively smooth texture and be primed in the usual fashion or purchased already primed. Stretched canvas can be printed on by laying the canvas on the floor and printing with a squeegee in the usual manner. If the canvas is too slack, and good close contact between the canvas and the screen cannot be maintained, newspapers should be placed between the floor and the canvas and used to support the canvas during printing. Unstretched canvas can be printed on a table or on the floor providing that the surface it rests on is smooth and level.

Regular oil-base or acrylic silk-screen inks or paints can be used for printing on canvas. For the painter who does not have a stock of silk-screen paints and who uses silk-screening techniques only occasionally, artists' oil tube colors mixed with transparent base can be substituted for the silk-screen paints.

5. Paints, Varnishes, and Other Printing Compounds

The artist owes a debt of gratitude to the commercial silk-screen industry and the manufacturers of silk-screen paints and equipment for the results of their years of research in the development of the process. Because of the demands of specialized industries and of commercial users, the manufacturers of silk-screen materials have provided an immense variety of paints for printing on virtually every type of material. The artist drawing from this vast wealth of material will find his horizons unlimited.

This chapter is meant to acquaint the reader with some of the major types of paints, also called process inks, and varnishes and fillers available. The type of paint is classified by the manner in which it dries. Three major types are in common use: those that dry by evaporation, those that dry by oxidation, and those that dry by polymerization.

EVAPORATION TYPE

This type of paint, drying by the evaporation of the solvents in the mixture, leaves a paint film on the printed surface. This is one of the largest categories, containing paint that will print on paper, cardboard, wood, foil, and most types of plastics.

Most of the paint used by artists is in this category, which includes paint that dries with a gloss or non-gloss, opaque or transparent color. Each varies in drying time from as little as 15 minutes to 1 or 2 hours. The drying of this type of paint can be accelerated by hot air and by special drying machines that dry the paint in seconds. The drying time of any paint will depend not only on its type, but also upon the climatic conditions and the surface it is printed on. Paint printed on glass will take longer to dry than paint printed on an absorbent surface such as paper. A wide variety of materials is available, however, to mix with the paint to hasten or to retard the drying time. Included in this category of evaporating paints are some interesting paints developed for specific uses. The following brief description may encourage the printmaker to expand his artistic potential by utilizing new materials.

5-1

Daylight Fluorescent Paint

The extremely vibrant, intense colors, primarily used for advertising and campaign posters, are now gaining a wider use in the arts. Formerly, they were thought to be too "garish" for the fine arts; now, however, that concept has been reversed with newer trends in painting. "Pop" and "Op" artists have exploited the brightness of the paints and put them to good use. Likewise, their use in printmaking has occurred with increasing frequency. There was a time when the fluorescents were very difficult to handle in the silk-screen process, but now they are as easy to print as any process color. They may even be mixed with other process colors to increase their brilliance.

Plastic Paint

These specially modified acrylic lacquers are designed for printing on acrylic, styrene, rigid vinyl, cellulose, and other plastics (Figure 5-1). Some of these paints can even undergo the process of vacuum forming after printing, by which they gain even greater adhesion to the plastic during the heat-forming process.

Vacuum forming, or "blister" packs, have been used for many years in packaging and advertisements of all sorts. The vacuum-forming process is simple in principle. A clear piece of plastic is heated until malleable and brought down over a shaping form. The air in the mold is sucked out by means of a vacuum and the heated plastic assumes the shape of the object or objects beneath it. Artists like Tom Wesselman and Claes Oldenberg have been exploring this new medium with exciting results. With editions of their prints that utilize vacuum-formed parts, they are helping to change the face of printmaking and broaden the scope of this art.

5-1. TEABAG, 39 by 29 inches, by Claes Oldenburg, 1965. Media: vacuum-formed Plexiglas, cloth object and silk-screen. Collection of the author. (Photograph by Neal Hall.)

Decal Lacquer

Decalcomania lacquer is used to print decalcomanias, popularly known as decals, or to print on cardboard and printing papers. The lacquer colors, which dry with a flexible, smooth film that will not crack when bent, are ideally suited for use on prints that will be folded into a three-dimensional form.

Decals have been used for years to transfer an image on surfaces ordinarily too difficult or inconvenient to print on. Commonly used for advertising schools and universities (school insignias, etc.), they have always fascinated me. They are relatively easy to make by applying lacquer or enamel paints to a gummed-paper surface. Then moistening the paper causes the lacquer image to slide off onto the desired surface. I began to explore the possibilities of the decal as an art form when I was working out the problems of printing on a glass cylinder. There are ways of printing directly on the glass by using a jig or wood support for the glass and a curved squeegee, but they are far too time consuming. In addition to the time factor, constant handling and rehandling of the glass makes it vulnerable to breakage, and a slight misregistration would cause the whole piece to be ruined. In this situation the decal functions at its best. The entire edition can be run on decal paper and when completed, transferred to the glass.

Decals can be made in three easy steps. One, a heavy coat of clear lacquer is printed on a water-soluble gummed-surface decal paper. Two, the image is printed on the dry lacquer surface. Three, another coat of clear lacquer printed over the entire decal makes a kind of lacquer "sandwich." Later, the decal is "slid off" the paper by immersing it in water for approximately 30 seconds — just enough time for the water to soak through the paper and soften the gummed surface beneath the lacquer. The decal is then removed from the water and the film slid off the paper onto the desired surface.

Since the paint has a lacquer base and lacquer solvents will be used to clean the paint from the screen, the stencil cannot be made of lacquer type cut-film. Photographic stencils, water-soluble cut-films, glue or prepared water-soluble blockout fillers may be used with the lacquer paints without any danger of being dissolved.

5-2. DECALCOMANIA REVISITED I, 19-inch circumference by 9 inches high, by Clifford T. Chieffo, 1966. Media: Prussian Blue lacquer silk-screened decal on glass. (Photograph by Clifford T. Chieffo.)

OXIDATION TYPE

Oxidation is a chemical reaction by which oxygen is combined with a material to create an entirely new material. This process occurs during the drying of some paint films, particularly those of oil-based paints. The solvents in the paint evaporate rather quickly and then oxidation begins to take place. Longer drying periods are usually necessary for this type of paint.

Oil-based process colors designed for printing on paper, cardboard, felt, and canvas awnings may be used for printing on the artist's canvas, if the canvas is primed in the usual manner to prevent the oils from rotting the canvas. Canvas awnings are not usually primed because they never last long enough for the action of the oil to have effect.

Enamel paint for printing on metal, wood, Masonite, glass, paper, and cardboard is included in this category of paints. Most enamels dry with a gloss and some with a high gloss. The high gloss enamels are usually utilized in exterior sign work. For high gloss and flexibility in the finished paint film, some companies use a percentage of synthetic base added to their paint. A clear coat of synthetic varnish can be screened on a thoroughly dried finished print to create deeper, richer color, to protect the surface, and to add a gloss finish.

Artists' tube colors would also come under the heading of oxidizing-type paints. Since they are oil-based they may be used in silk-screen work to print any water-soluble stencil. The artists' tube colors are considerably more concentrated than most process colors; therefore, for the tube colors to have the proper consistency for printing they must be mixed with transparent base. Because the mixing process is important, the following procedure should be used.

A. Take a small amount (one rounded tablespoon) of transparent base and place it on a glass palette.

B. Mix the tube color into the transparent base until the mixture is uniform. From time to time spread the base thinly on the palette with a spatula to see if any concentrated color is still unmixed.

C. When this mass is uniform, more transparent base may be added to extend the quantity necessary for printing. A small color test should be made on a scrap of the printing stock to determine just how transparent the color is. If it is too transparent, more tube color may be added to a small amount of the color mass. When the mixture is uniform, it is mixed with the remaining amount. If the color is not transparent enough, more transparent base can be added.

The artist will find tube colors expensive if he does a fair amount of printing. Their use should be reserved for colors that are unavailable in the screen process line.

POLYMERIZATION TYPE

Polymerization is the process of forming a polymer, or of combining two or more molecules into a single larger molecule. This relatively small group of paints is used to print on difficult surfaces such as glass, ceramics, metals, polyesters, and silicones. They are generally known as epoxy or epoxy resin paints. Some types need a catalyst added to the paint just before it is used to begin the drying action. Others need to be "baked" or heated at a given temperature in order to "cure" or dry the paint. This type of paint is seldom used by the artist. If he does use it he should follow the directions of the manufacturer scrupulously, and particularly any safety precautions that may be given.

OTHER PRINTING COMPOUNDS

An occasion may arise when an artist wishes to combine two print media. Printing on a lithograph stone or an etching plate with a particular silk-screen stencil creates effects that would not be possible if either one of the media were used singly. For example, the artist may have a photographic stencil of a photograph already on a screen and he may wish to integrate this with a very delicately shaded lithographic image. All he need do to combine the two images is to screen print directly on the grease sensitive stone with lithographic asphaltum, a greasy substance with a creamy consistency. The lithographic stone would then be processed in the usual manner.

In another example of combined print media, the artist might have an interesting negative stencil on a screen and wish to combine this with an etching plate. He can print the stencil directly on the etching plate with material resistant to acid. Asphaltum, or a specially prepared material used in industry for printing an acid resist on printed circuits that will be etched, can be used. A silk-screen supply house can provide you with this material in ready-to-use form. Once the material is printed on the plate, the rest of the etching process is continued as usual.

Bronze inks and powders

Printing with metallic paint is easily achieved by using bronze powders or bronze ink. Bronze powders come in many colors of which light and dark gold, silver, copper bronze, and aluminum are but a few. The artist is able to control the exact color of the mixture by adjusting the quantity of powder added to the bronze vehicle or varnish, and by mixing two colors of powder together in the varnish. Almost every line or series of paint type will have a varnish suitable for use with the bronze powder. It is recommended that the proper type of varnish be used to carry the powder, especially when the printing surface is other than paper and cardboard. Manufacturers' directions should be followed for the suggested ratio of powder to varnish, and for drying times. An approximate ratio, however, for most paints would be $1/2$ pound of powder to 1 quart of bronze vehicle or varnish.

Gold and silver inks, ready-mixed, are supplied by some manufacturers for use on paper and cardboard. The manufacturer may recommend the use of number 12 silk, or coarser, depending upon the particle size of the bronze powder.

Varnishes and Thinners

Overprint varnishes are available to protect the final print surface and to add a gloss. They also serve to make the color appear richer and more intense. Most varnishes are clear and will not affect the colors in the print. The paint should be absolutely dry before any final varnish is applied.

Binding varnish is designed to be mixed with certain color series to create a greater adhesion of the paint film to surfaces that are absorbent. The varnish also prevents the vehicle in the paint from soaking into the surface of the stock and causing the paint to dry with a powdery film which can be rubbed off.

Transparent base extends the paint, makes it more transparent, and aids in the printing of fine detail. Transparent base, both gloss and nongloss, is a paste of alumina (aluminum oxide) stearate ground in the same vehicle as the paint for which it is intended. Extender base also extends the paint, but it will not change the viscosity of the paint with which it is mixed. There is an opaque base that is designed to extend opaque paints in commercial printing, but the inexpensive, milky-white paste is seldom needed in silk-screen printing in the fine arts.

Several thinners in addition to mineral spirits can speed up or slow down the drying time of the paint. Retarding thinner is used to slow down the drying time of the paint. This thinner, useful when fine detail is printed with a fine mesh screen, prevents the paint from drying on the screen and clogging the mesh. To accelerate the drying time, a reducing thinner should be used. Termed reducing because it "reduces" the drying time of the paint or ink, the thinner can cut the drying time of a paint in half. Xylol, a derivative of coal tar, also makes an excellent reducing thinner. Note, be sure to provide adequate ventilation and fire precautions in the studio when using large amounts of any thinner. Most of them are very flammable and their fumes may be toxic. As usual, always check the recommendations of the manufacturer before adding any varnishes, oils, or thinners to any paint or extender base. Manufacturers vary widely on the type and amount of any substance added to their products. In general, thinners should be used with discretion because too much of any thinner will considerably weaken the structure of the paint film.

CONSISTENCY AND PAINT STORAGE

The printing consistency for most paints should resemble heavy cream. Paint mixed with transparent base, however, will have a heavier "body" and need not be thinned to the consistency of cream. If the transparent base mixture sticks to the squeegee during printing, it may be thinned with mineral spirits. When any paint mixture proves to need thinning, the entire amount should be removed from the screen and placed in the mixing can or on the palette for the addition of the thinner. In this manner, the total paint supply will be kept homogenous.

Excess paint may be stored in covered jars, new metal "soft" margarine containers, or cans covered with plastic food wrap for many weeks or months. Generally, the pigment will settle to the bottom of the container and the vehicle left covering the top will prevent the mixture from drying out. Some artists prefer to add a small amount of varnish to the top of the mixture without stirring it. The varnish then dries with a protective film which prevents the paint mixture from hardening. When it is time to reuse the paint, the varnish skin is removed and the paint is thinned and made ready for printing.

6. The Use of Silk-Screen Printing in Schools

Silk-screen printing, as a graphic art process, can be an important facet of the general art education curriculum in the elementary, junior high, and high school. Aside from its obvious usefulness in the upper grades for making posters, stage set decorations, programs, signs, etc., its potential as a fine art medium should be considered. The building of the equipment, the planning, and the execution of the print offers the student a wide range of challenging experiences. In the high school where oil-based paints are available, the Maskoid water-soluble stencil and paper stencil methods will probably be the easiest to handle. Where water paints are used, i.e., in the elementary school, stencils should be of wax paper or oak tag. All of the usual procedures can be followed. For schools with fewer facilities and a minimal amount of money in the art budget, the following suggestions and hints are offered.

SCREEN MATERIALS

Inexpensive organdy may be substituted for silk whenever oil-based paints are used. However, the screen should be of silk if the printing is to be done with water-based paints. Organdy tends to absorb water, which causes the material to go slack during printing.

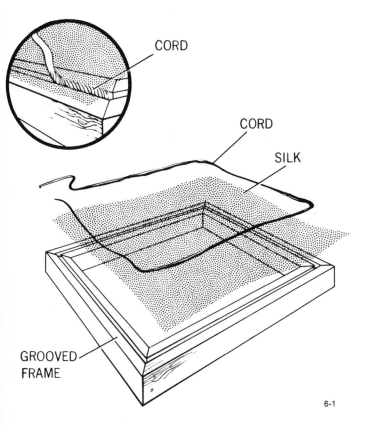

CORD

CORD

SILK

GROOVED FRAME

6-1

STRETCHING TECHNIQUES AND FRAMES

For frequent replacement of the silk or organdy a "tackless" stretching method is recommended.

When the screens are made in the school shop or classroom, one side is grooved with a groove-cutter, router, or table saw before the parts are assembled. An $1/8$ by $3/8$-inch groove is adequate. Using a miter-cut corner, assemble the parts and join them with screws. The silk is laid over the screen covering the grooves and is held in place by a few tacks in each corner. A fiber cord or waxed twine forced down into the grooves stretches the silk taut. Then remove the tacks and trim the excess silk from the frame (Figure 6-1). A wedge may be used to tamp the tight fitting cord into the groove, or a mechanical wedger designed for this purpose is available at most silk-screen supply houses. Strips of wood dowels may be substituted for the cord. When the silk needs replacement, the cord or dowel is pulled from the groove and the silk is freed.

For an introduction to the stencil-making process in the elementary school, various simple screen frames can be built.

For example, different sizes of embroidery hoops may be successfully used as small screen frames since they are easily handled by young children. The silk is stretched over the hoop in the same fashion as cloth would be for embroidering.

Half-inch plywood may also be used for a frame if a square or rectangular section is cut out from its center. The silk can be stretched in the usual manner and held with tacks, or it can be held temporarily with tacks and glued to the plywood with hot wood glue. When the glue is dry the tacks can be removed. The inside edge of the screen can be taped and sealed with a coat of shellac (Figure 6-2).

For the early elementary grades, heavy cardboard or the top of a shoe box or shirt box can be used as a frame in lieu of wood. Cut out a rectangular shape in the box top and stretch the silk over the opening. Attach the silk with staples or glue. Tape all the exposed cardboard areas with 2-inch gummed-paper tape and apply several coats of shellac.

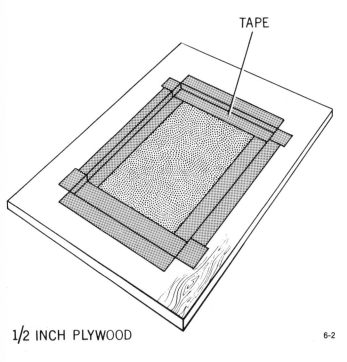

TAPE

1/2 INCH PLYWOOD

6-2

PAINTS

For easier clean-up, and when silk is used as the screen material, water-based paints should be used instead of oil-based paints. For elementary schools, use poster or tempera paints mixed with household corn starch or powdered soap for thickening. This mixture will suffice for limited printing, but the solution has a tendency to clog the mesh. Heavier mesh silk, 10xx or 12xx, will help, but for true nonclogging properties it is better to buy a special plasticizer base made to mix with tempera. The plasticizer is a material with the consistency of butter that is mixed in a one to one ratio with poster or tempera paints. Water-based silk-screen inks are available in a wide range of colors if your school budget permits their purchase.

When using water-based paints, remember that the blockout material must be impervious to water. Lacquer filler, lacquer stencils (cut-film), photo stencils and wax paper stencils can be used for stencil materials without being damaged or ruined by water paints.

SOLVENTS

Mineral spirits or varsol should be used for cleaning oil-based paints from the screen because of their low cost and less toxic fumes.

SQUEEGEES

For elementary school printing, rubber floor tiles can be substituted for the regular squeegee. Linoleum and floor covering shops can usually supply you with sundry scraps at reduced rates. They can be cut to size with a mat knife. Tongue depressors and stiff cardboard can also be used as squeegees.

CAUTION! Observe the labels on all cans that may contain toxic substances. Keep the classrooms where these materials are used well ventilated. Exhaust fans should be used whenever available or several windows kept open. All paint and solvent soaked rags should be stored in a covered metal container and properly disposed of each day. A fire extinguisher should be kept close at hand.

Glossary

ACETONE
A volatile solvent formed in the distillation of acetates.

ACRYLIC
A type of synthetic resin formed by the polymerization of acrylic acid esters. Sold under common trade names — Lucite or Plexiglas.

BASEBOARD
A flat, smooth surface, usually a table or a separate piece of wood to which the screen frame is attached for printing.

BRAYER
A rubber roller used in printmaking to spread the ink on a wood block or lithograph stone.

CATALYST
The substance that accelerates a chemical change.

COLLAGE
A composition composed of various textured materials such as paper, cloth, wood, etc.

COUNTERSINK BIT
A tool to bore a cone-shaped opening to admit the cone-shaped head of a screw.

DRILL BIT
A tool for boring round holes.

DUROMETER
A unit of measure as read on a durometer, a testing device for calculating the indentation hardness of rubber.

EPOXY
A binding substance and adhesive used in paint mediums.

FREE-PIN HINGE
See "slip-pin hinges."

GLAZING
The process of building up a surface of thin, transparent paint layers.

HINGEBAR
A strip of wood attached to the baseboard by means of adjustable bolts to which the screen frame is hinged.

JIG
A device for holding the work during the printing operation.

KILN-DRIED
Wood that has been dried in a kiln or large oven.

LITHOGRAPHER'S CRAYON
See "tusche."

MESH COUNT
The number of threads per square inch in a given screen material.

MINERAL SPIRITS
A petroleum distillate used as a solvent and thinner for paint.

PLASTICIZER
Substances added to brittle paints to make them more flexible.

PLEXIGLAS
A thermoplastic notable for its transparency.

POLYESTERS
A class of synthetic resins.

PRIMED CANVAS
Cotton or linen cloth that has been prepared with a surface or ground suitable for painting.

PRINTED CIRCUIT
A rigid board supporting a diagram or circuit of a conductor of electricity. A component in radios, television sets, etc.

PROP
A leg of wood or metal attached to the screen frame to hold it off the baseboard.

REGISTRATION TABS
Paper or metal guides on the baseboard to aid in positioning the printing stock.

RIGID VINYL
A thermoplastic material formed by polymerization.

ROSS BOARD
Trade name for an embossed cardboard.

RULING PEN
An adjustable pointed pen used by draftsmen and architects.

SCREEN FRAME
A wood or metal support to which silk or other suitable screen material is attached.

SHAPED CANVAS
Canvas that is stretched over a three-dimensional frame structure, and then painted upon.

SHIM
A thin strip of material, cardboard, metal, etc. used to raise the level of the hingebar.

SIZING
A gelatinous preparation made from glue or starch that is coated on a fabric to give it body.

SLIP-PIN HINGE
A hinge which is held together with a removable pin or shaft.

SQUEEGEE
A printing tool composed of a handle and a rubber blade that forces the printing paint through the screen mesh.

STENCIL
Any material that blocks the passage of paint through the screen.

STRETCHER BARS
Wood strips cut with tongue and groove mitered corners and with beveled sides used to support canvas for painting.

STYRENE
A transparent thermoplastic formed by the polymerization of styrene.

TUSCHE
A greasy or waxy stick, or liquid substance used in lithographic and silk-screen processes.

VEHICLE
The medium or liquid used as the carrier of pigments in paint.

WOOD VISE
A vise or clamp with protected or covered jaws that will not mar the surface of the object held.

Bibliography

Fossett, Robert O., *Techniques in Photography for the Silk Screen Printer*, Cincinnati, Ohio, Signs of the Times Publishing Company, 1959.

Hiett, Harry L., *57 How-To-Do-It Charts*, Cincinnati, Ohio, Signs of the Times Publishing Company, 1959.

Kosloff, Albert, *Photographic Screen Process Printing*, Cincinnati, Ohio, Signs of the Times Publishing Company.

Mayer, Ralph, *The Artist's Handbook*, New York, New York, The Viking Press, Inc., Revised Edition, 1957.

Shokler, Harry, *Artist's Manual for Silk Screen Print Making*, New York, New York, Tudor Publishing Company, 1960.

Index